# BIRTH, MARRIAGE AND DEATH RECORDS

## FAMILY HISTORY FROM PEN & SWORD

# CONTENTS

# INTRODUCTION

Today, no single group has a greater, more active interest in records of births, marriages and deaths than the vast army of people who are researching their family histories. Family historians represent by far the biggest users of parish and civil registers and, as the interest in family history research continues to grow, there is no sign that this situation is about to change. But how many researchers take the time to stop and think about the records that they use? How many of us ask why the records were created in the first place? And how many family historians can say that they fully understand the processes behind their creation?

This book is designed to guide researchers through the records and explain how and where to access them, but it also seeks to tell the fascinating story behind the records that we use in our everyday research.

It is the story of the attempts of successive administrations to maintain an accurate and comprehensive record of the births, marriages and deaths of the inhabitants of the British Isles – a story that stretches back through nearly 500 years of British history, covering a period that saw the country develop from a medieval state dominated by the Church to a modern industrialised nation. It is a story of challenges and innovations; of successes and failures; of starts and stops but, ultimately, it is a story of how the present-day civil registration systems in force in the different parts of Britain have come to rank among the most comprehensive and efficient in the world.

Nowadays, registering the birth of a newborn child is seen as an integral part of everyday life; similarly, a visit to the local Register Office is an important part of the process of dealing with the death of a loved one; and for couples getting married, the signing of the register is one of the central parts of the ceremony. This is also the story of how we reached this position.

We will see how the beginnings of our civil registration system can be traced back to the period when the Church of England was first established under King Henry VIII. The Church (then inseparable from the State) was the first of many organisations and institutions to take an interest in the registration process. Over the years, politicians, statisticians, religious Dissenters and members of the legal and medical professions have all attempted to exert their influence on how the system is run and to have their ideas incorporated in the process.

Successive pieces of legislation resulted in a steady shift towards a more comprehensive system, as loopholes were closed and coverage was gradually extended, but it is probably fair to say that fully comprehensive coverage will never be achieved. There will always be certain groups or individuals living on the fringes of society who, whether through ignorance or wilful deceit, will manage to evade the system's net.

The importance of the legislation in telling our story cannot be underestimated. The various Acts and Bills give us a fascinating glimpse into the minds of the people who created them, highlighting their intentions – which, as we will see, were often far removed from the realities of their applications. It is all too easy, with hindsight, to see how ill-equipped the Church of England was to fulfil its designated role as official State record keeper, but it was a role that the Church held for 300 years.

One of the biggest problems facing the authorities, Church and State alike, has always been how to inform themselves that an event has taken place. The ultimate responsibility for registering events has shifted over the years from the record keeper to the citizen and the punishment for failing to do what was required of both parties has likewise varied.

As the British Empire grew, the authorities faced a fresh challenge – how to record the births, marriages and deaths of British citizens who were living and working in the colonies and dependencies in the four corners of the world. And there are always new challenges around the corner. The General Register Office now keeps records of events occurring overseas, at sea, in the air and even onboard hovercrafts.

The idea of civil registration had been discussed for many years before it was eventually introduced. The delay in its introduction was largely brought about by those with a vested interest in maintaining the old system and the Act that was eventually passed in 1836 (and brought in the following year) fell some way short of what had originally been proposed. Historians are left to ponder what might have been.

And this is a theme that runs throughout the story – the expansive ideas of progressive thinkers constantly being thwarted by the establishment. But we need to keep an open mind here – we should be thankful that the records were created in the first place and that their survival rate is actually, all things considered, very good. With the exception of the decade of civil war that affected the whole of the British Isles in the middle of the seventeenth century, the past 500 years have been a period of remarkable domestic stability.

From time to time the spectre of taxation raised its ugly head but raising money was only rarely at the heart of the registration process. In the early years, it was the need to provide proof of identity for legal purposes that was the main driver; later, the ever-growing army of economists and social planners wanted the information for a variety of statistical purposes.

Providing the service is an expensive process but successive governments have never found it hard to justify the expenditure. Unlike our decennial census, the civil registration system is not under any kind of threat. Indeed, the challenge of providing the service in an online environment continues to breathe new life into a system which is now over 170 years old.

*Chapter 1*

# PARISH REGISTERS, PART 1:
## 'Every Weddyng Christenyng and Buryeng'

T he pages of our history books are crammed full of memorable dates: the Battle of Hastings (1066) and the Battle of Bosworth (1485); the outbreak of the English Civil War (1642); the Great Fire of London (1666); and the two world wars (1914–18 and 1939–45). The world of family history research has its own set of important dates and it could be argued that none is more significant than 1538. Indeed, it could be said that family history began on 5 September 1538, the date of the order issued by Thomas Cromwell requiring 'every parson vicar or curate' to keep a register recording 'every weddyng christenyng and buryeng' occurring within his parish. Without parish registers providing the vital information concerning our ancestors' births, marriages and deaths, it's difficult to see how family history could be a viable pursuit.

Parish registers are still maintained by churches today and, although their role as the primary means of civil registration may have been eroded over the centuries, their longevity alone represents a quite remarkable achievement. There can be few aspects of our everyday lives that have survived as long and are still going strong nearly 500 years on.

Thomas Cromwell was appointed to the role of Vicar-General by Henry VIII in 1535. As Henry's Chief Minister, and with the full support of the king behind him, Cromwell had already played a key role in establishing and reforming the Church of England. In addition, although not recognised as such at the time, his scheme for introducing a form of civil registration of births, marriages and deaths turned out to be one of the most significant acts of his relatively short tenure.

## Thomas Cromwell, Earl of Essex

Nobody knows when Thomas Cromwell was born. He is thought to have been born in Putney, Surrey sometime around 1485. The fact that historians are so vague about this is significant, as it was Cromwell himself who introduced parish registers to England and Wales in 1538. Before this date, there is simply nothing to record the dates of the vital events in the lives of ordinary people.

Cromwell came from a relatively humble background. His father, Walter Cromwell, was a blacksmith and cloth merchant in Putney. Thomas's early life is not well documented, although he later told Thomas Cranmer, the Archbishop of Canterbury, that he had been a 'ruffian' in his youth.

*Thomas Cromwell, from the painting (in the School of Holbein) at the National Portrait Gallery.* (J Charles Cox, *Parish Registers of England*, 1910)

As a young man, Cromwell left home and travelled to the Continent, joining the French Army and fighting at the Battle of Garigliano in Italy in 1503. He later made his way to the Netherlands where he met up with a group of English merchants and found work in the cloth trade.

Cromwell made many useful contacts during his time in Holland and when he returned to England and married a widow, Elizabeth Williams, the daughter of Henry Wykys, he was soon able to set himself up in business as a cloth merchant.

By 1520, Cromwell had branched out and, despite a lack of any formal legal training, established himself as a lawyer in London. He began to work for influential clients including Charles Knyvett, a surveyor to the Duke of Buckingham, and his name became increasingly well known and respected.

Cromwell entered Parliament in 1523 and was soon befriended by Cardinal Wolsey, King Henry VIII's closest advisor. When Wolsey fell from the king's favour in 1529, Cromwell was initially concerned that he would fall with him, but he soon won the king's trust and by 1531 had been appointed Henry's Chief Minister.

It was almost certainly Cromwell's experience in Italy and the Netherlands and his first-hand knowledge of record-keeping practices on the Continent that inspired his order of 5 September 1538, which led to the introduction of parish registers in England and Wales.

On 18 April 1540 Cromwell became the 1st Earl of Essex and at the same time was appointed to the role of Lord Great Chamberlain, but his fall from grace was even more rapid than his rise to fame and fortune had been. Just two months later, Cromwell was arrested and imprisoned in the Tower of London, accused of treason and heresy. He was beheaded on Tower Hill on 28 July 1540 without a trial, and his head was put on show on London Bridge.

The king appears to have regretted Cromwell's execution, later referring to him as 'the most faithful servant he ever had'.

Thomas Cromwell's sister Katherine married a Welshman named Morgan Williams. Their son Richard, who changed his name to Cromwell, was the great-grandfather of Oliver Cromwell, the Lord Protector.

Dictionary of National Biography
www.oxforddnb.com/view/article/6769

The full text of the order makes fascinating reading (see Appendix). It contains all the key elements of the record keeping that we're so familiar with today but it also shows a surprisingly modern-sounding concern for the safe-keeping and security of the registers. The order can also be seen as significant for the measure of its impact on the day-to-day lives of ordinary people; its intrusiveness is unusual for a time when the majority of legislation tended to deal with important matters of State, largely affecting the Church and the nobility. It is a relatively rare example in medieval times of the State taking an interest in the affairs of tradesmen, craftsmen, artisans and labourers – particularly when this interest had nothing to do with taxation.

At a time when the word of the Church and State was absolute law, it is perhaps understandable that there was little or no open resistance to Cromwell's order, but it's also true that there was some disquiet in the country in the latter half of the 1530s as rumours of the advent of this new legislation spread. The fear of increased taxation was never too far away from people's minds and although the published order contained no mention of a revenue-raising element, it's clear that the threat of a future amendment hung over the populace and caused concern around the country.

Evidence of this concern survives in the English Domestic State Papers (Domestic State Papers, Henry VIII, vol. 14, pt 1, nos 295, 507, 815). John Marshall, the vicar of South Carlton in Nottinghamshire, referring to the new arrangements in February 1539, expressed the widespread fear that 'paymentes should or myght grow uppon them at lengthe to the kyngs hyghnes'.

So if Cromwell's motivation wasn't financial, what was behind the introduction of the order? The wording of the order gives its purpose as being 'for the avancement of the trewe honor of almighty God, encrease of vertu and discharge of the kynges majestie …', which seems to suggest that it was all a part of the bigger campaign to impose the authority of the newly established Church. But the truth is that we can't be certain.

What we do know is that Cromwell spent much of his early life in the Netherlands where the Spanish rulers had introduced baptismal registers in the late 1400s. This new concept of keeping a record of life events would certainly have come to Cromwell's attention and he would have been quick to see the advantages of operating such a system in a modern state.

The issuing of Cromwell's order came at a time that very neatly marks the transition of England from a medieval state into a modern one. The newly formed Anglican Church had a new responsibility – one that it was to hold for the next 300 years.

It would be nice to report that the instructions contained in the order were implemented uniformly and consistently throughout the country; that the registers have always been looked after and cared for in a proper manner and that, therefore, in every parish in England and Wales we will find a continuous run of parish registers going back to 1538. Unfortunately, this is far from the truth. In fact there are known to be fewer than a thousand surviving registers that date back to 1538 or 1539 – this represents roughly one out of every ten English and Welsh parishes. And the vast majority of these registers are transcripts made around the turn of the seventeenth century rather than originals dating from the time of Henry VIII.

Remarkably, a small number of registers have survived from before the date of Cromwell's order. This shows that the idea of registering baptisms, marriages and burials was not an entirely alien one: what was new was the concept of introducing such a system on a national scale and making the keeping of parish registers a legal requirement.

In 1831 a survey was carried out of the registers then held in parish churches throughout England and Wales. The results were published in a 'Blue Book' in 1833, but unfortunately the work doesn't seem to have been conducted with a great deal of care, and a number of errors were made – errors that have since been republished and taken as fact. The Blue Book lists as many as forty registers that begin before 1538 but on closer examination this turns out to be highly inaccurate. John Charles Cox, writing in 1910 in his seminal work, *The Parish Registers of England* (p. 235), suggests that 'the large majority of the forty set forth in the Blue Book prove on investigation to be but moonshine'. Figures were misread by the clergy (whether knowingly or not) which attributed far earlier dates to their registers than is in fact the case.

Cox concludes that the actual number was 'less than half the number named in the 1833 Blue Book'. Unfortunately, even he appears

*Tipton Parish Register with entries from 1573–7 incorrectly transcribed as 1513–17. The register is held by Staffordshire Record Office.* (J Charles Cox, *Parish Registers of England*, 1910) to overstate the number of pre-Cromwellian registers. His assertion that the parish register of Tipton, Staffordshire constitutes 'by far the most remarkable of these early instances' with entries starting in 1513, turns out to be yet another instance of 'moonshine'. Recent research has shown that the entries actually begin in 1573 and that the error was the result of a later mistranscription.

Cox also refers to the registers of Altham, Lancashire starting in 1518 but this too seems to be wishful thinking. The registers of the two neighbouring parishes of Perlethorpe and Carburton in Nottinghamshire, both of which commence in 1528, may in fact contain the earliest authenticated entries, but even these, as Cox points out, seem to have been made retrospectively. Both refer to entries being made 'since' the year 1528 suggesting that they were written up some years after the event. And this practice of copying older entries into a new register – together with all the attendant issues associated with transcription and mistranscription – is one that continued throughout the sixteenth century, and sometimes much later.

Thomas Cromwell barely survived to see his registration scheme implemented. He was executed for treason in 1540 after falling out with Henry over the king's disastrous marriage to Anne of Cleves. Henry himself lived just another seven years and one of the earliest acts of his son Edward's regime was to reissue Cromwell's order for keeping parish registers. The order was repeated virtually word-for-word but the very fact that it was deemed necessary to do this gives us clear evidence that its terms were not being universally observed.

The religious upheavals of Queen Mary's reign and the early years of Queen Elizabeth I do not seem to have had a major impact on the standards of record keeping. Surviving parish registers from the period tend to continue without any noticeable changes, despite the occasional comments from ministers on both sides of the religious divide.

The next major development in the history of parish registers came when a 'further order' was made in 1597 (later embodied in the seventieth canon in 1603). This legislation attempted to rectify some of the problems that had developed over the previous sixty years. One of the main shortcomings of Cromwell's order was that no explicit instructions had been given regarding the qualities of the register itself. For the sake of economy most ministers had, understandably, opted to purchase cheap paper registers but it had soon become clear that these were generally not up to the job and by the end of the sixteenth century many had deteriorated or even disintegrated. Elizabeth's order now stipulated that 'every Parish Church and Chapel within this Realm shall be provided one Parchment Book at the charge of the Parish' – the key word here being 'parchment'.

Recognising that most of the existing paper registers were in a perilous condition, the order also required parishes to copy the earlier entries (from the date of Queen Elizabeth's accession in 1558) into the new parchment books. Note that they were not asked to copy any details from before 1558 and it's for this reason that so many of the surviving registers start from this later date rather than the date of Cromwell's order in 1538.

The 1597 order included another requirement that has had a huge impact on the world of family history research. The churchwardens of each parish were ordered to send 'copies of the registers … annually, within one month of Easter … to the register of the diocese, that they might be faithfully preserved in the Episcopal archives'. These copies are commonly known as 'Bishop's Transcripts' and, where they have survived, can be invaluable to historians, particularly in cases where the original registers have been lost or damaged.

But their main purpose was to provide a check against fraudulent entries being made in the registers themselves. The temptation to tamper with parish registers must have been felt by many people through the years – parents who wanted to alter a date of baptism to legitimise a child, or to create an entry for a marriage that never took place, or those who wanted to do the opposite, to destroy the evidence of the baptism of an older brother or to remove the record of an earlier marriage.

The Bishop's Transcripts, safely housed many miles distant from the parish church, provided legal evidence of what was originally entered in the registers. However, the survival rate of the transcripts is not good and the quality of the records is generally unsatisfactory. Edward James Boyce, the rector of Houghton, Hampshire, writing in 1895, observed that the 'latter part of this Canon (70) has been so negligently obeyed by the ministers and Churchwardens, and by the

Registrars of the Dioceses in their care of the transcripts sent to them, that nothing in most cases can be more valueless than the Diocesan Registers as duplicates'.

So despite these new directions, the standards of record-keeping continued to fall far short of what we would consider appropriate today. Many ministers and churchwardens were in the habit of making notes of baptisms, marriages and burials on loose sheets of paper which would later be copied into the registers. It's not hard to see how these could become misplaced or how mistakes could be made when transcribing the details.

When incumbents became old or ill (or both) the record-keeping business of the parish could often become neglected. Most lengthy gaps in registers can be attributed directly to these circumstances and despite the best efforts of the incoming minister it was usually impossible to rectify the situation completely. It's not at all uncommon to find notes in the registers made by ministers commenting on the shortcomings of their predecessors.

Sometimes the gaps were only identified many years later. In 1799 Samuel Horsfall, the newly appointed curate of Wendling in Norfolk, made the following entry: 'XI. April 1799. On which day the register books were brought to me at my house in Gressenhall when it appeared a period of 40 years is missing from the Reg$^r$. of Baptisms. Viz. from 1678 to 1718.' Horsfall seems to have been a meticulous and conscientious record keeper. He was also responsible for a census taken of the inhabitants of Wells, Norfolk in 1793.

The entries in these early registers tend to be brief in nature. Baptisms frequently record just the date of the event, the Christian name of the child and the name and surname of the father; marriages are unlikely to show more than the names of the two parties getting married; and more often than not burials show just the name of the deceased. Locations within the parish are only rarely given and useful genealogical information is somewhat thin on the ground. To our modern eyes this may seem particularly deficient but we have to see it all in the context of the times. For the purposes of a late-medieval society where the vast majority of the population lived in relatively small towns and villages or even in remote settlements, these details were generally all that was required. The minister knew who everyone was and could scarcely have comprehended that anyone would be remotely interested in the entries 400 years later.

Most of the early parish registers are what are known as 'composite' registers – that is, combined registers of baptisms, marriages and burials. Only the larger parishes would have been able to justify the cost of acquiring separate registers to record the three different events. Some composite registers have separate sections for baptisms, marriages and burials but many list all three together as they occur, usually with a marginal note indicating the type of entry.

The use of Latin in sixteenth-century registers is, unfortunately for modern researchers, widespread, but since the entries tend to be of a highly formulaic nature this doesn't present too many obstacles. By the early part of the seventeenth century, and particularly after the Civil War, English almost entirely replaced Latin as the language of choice for parish registers. Cox, in *The Parish Registers of England* (1910, p. 13), quotes an entry dating from 1610 made by Richard Kilbie, the minister of All Saint's, Derby, who saw 'no reason why a Register of English people should be written in Latin'.

By the time of Elizabeth's death, the Church of England's role as record keeper was well and truly established. Even if some of the registers haven't survived, practically every parish in England and Wales was keeping records of the baptisms, marriages and burials occurring in their area of jurisdiction. The registers were generally well kept and looked after by efficient and competent parish officials. Churchwardens were (in theory) sending annual copies of the entries in the registers to the diocesan archives and, as the Tudor dynasty gave way to the Stuarts, everything was running relatively smoothly.

## Chapter 2

# PARISH REGISTERS, PART 2:
## 'A True and Just Account … of All Sorts of Persons within the Commonwealth'

B y the time of the outbreak of the English Civil War, parish registers had been a part of everyday life in England and Wales for over a hundred years. The initial fear that the Crown planned to use the system as a means of raising revenue had been shown to be unfounded (for the time being at least), and any genuine resistance to the concept of registering life events had all but disappeared.

The first half of the seventeenth century was a time of growing religious and political disquiet. In 1642, the unrest that had been simmering since the accession of the Stuart dynasty in 1603 turned into full-scale rebellion when King Charles I, whose dealings with Parliament had become increasingly confrontational, attempted to arrest five MPs for treason.

Religion and politics in seventeenth-century England were inseparable and while the main causes of the Civil War may have been essentially political, there was also a strong religious component to the rebellion. Initially, the greatest impact of the Civil War on registration was a purely practical one. The upheaval caused by living in a country at war with itself would naturally disrupt many day-to-day processes and it's perhaps understandable at a time like this that keeping accurate and comprehensive records of baptisms, marriages and burials was not everyone's highest priority. And as the Puritan influence behind the Parliamentarian cause began to grow, clergymen who didn't see eye to eye with the new regime were routinely ejected from their parishes – a situation that led to yet more disruption in the record-keeping process.

The tumultuous nature of life in England and Wales during the Civil War and the Commonwealth period that followed has given rise to a phenomenon known in family history circles as 'the Commonwealth Gap'. While the registers from a particular parish may have been perfectly maintained up until the 1640s and just as well kept after the Restoration, it is not at all uncommon to find a significant gap in the records in the intervening period.

And yet this should have been a golden age for registration. An ordinance dating from 1644 reinforced Elizabeth's earlier order, requiring

> the minister and other officers of the church [to record] the names of all children baptized, and of their parents, and the time of their birth and baptizing ... and also the names of all persons married there and the time of their marriage; and also the names of all persons buried in that parish, and the time of their death and burial ...

It's worth noting that the requirement here was to record the *times* of these events in addition to the date – a requirement that seems to have been almost universally ignored. Also, that the dates of birth and death were supposed to be recorded – earlier legislation had always referred just to baptisms and burials.

Then, in 1653, the Commonwealth Government took the extra-ordinary step of taking the process out of the hands of the Church and setting up an early form of civil registration. An Act passed that year ordered that officers should be appointed (known, somewhat confusingly, as Parish Registers) with the task of ensuring 'that a true and just account might always be kept, of all marriages, and also of the births of children, and deaths of all sorts of persons within the commonwealth'. The Act also introduced an even more radical change – all marriages were now to be performed before a Justice of the Peace. The wording was quite clear: 'no other Marriage whatsoever within the Commonwealth of England, after the 29th of September, in the year One thousand six hundred fifty three, shall be held or accompted a Marriage according to the Laws of England'.

In most cases, the register books were simply handed over to the new civil authorities and contemporary evidence of this process is found throughout the registers themselves. In Hanwell, Middlesex

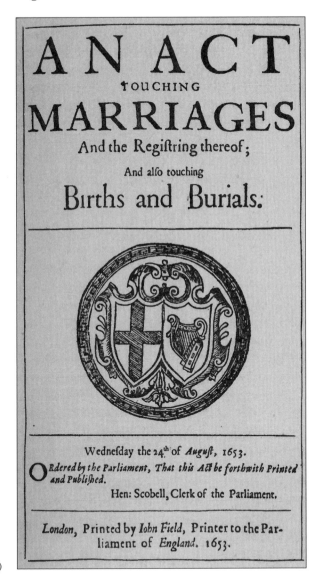

*The 1653 'Act touching Marriages and the Registring thereof ...' introduced a form of civil registration.* (J Charles Cox, Parish Registers of England, 1910)

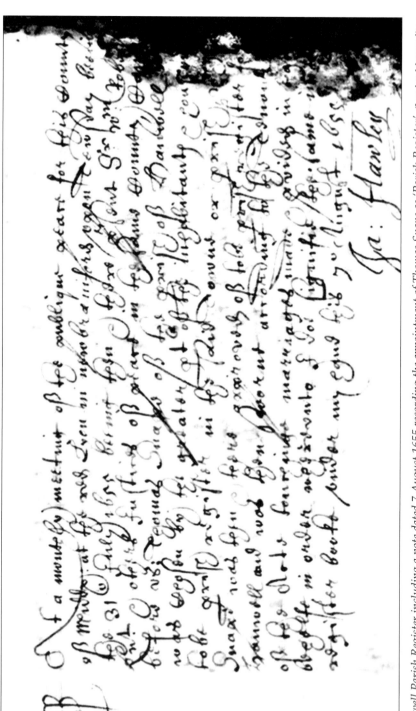

Hanwell Parish Register including a note dated 7 August 1655 recording the appointment of Thomas Snape as 'Parish Register'. (London Metropolitan Archives DRO/006/1).

there is a note dated 7 August 1655 recording the appointment of Thomas Snape as 'Parish Register'. Mr Snape was 'chosen by the greater part of the inhabitants and householders' of Hanwell at a meeting held at the Red Lyon, New Brainford (Brentford) on 31 July.

The entries continue in the Hanwell register without an apparent break. On 16 February 1657, the marriage of the Parish Register's son Thomas Snape junior to Sara Hoggray, daughter of John Hoggray, is recorded, with far more detail than might be expected. Besides the welcome addition of the fathers' names, we learn that the couple were married at 'Brainford' before a Justice and 'after ward in Brainford Church' – clear evidence that two ceremonies took place.

Unfortunately for family historians, this sort of detail is not typical and the new secular system was not a success. Whether the records were not kept efficiently at the time or whether they were lost as a result of the upheavals of the period isn't always clear. What is evident is that gaps in the registers continue to be commonplace after 1653.

In 1660, at the Restoration of the monarchy, the old ecclesiastical system was reintroduced and responsibility was placed back into the hands of the clergy. One of the first acts of the new regime was to confirm the legitimacy of all 'marriages by Justices' which had taken place since 1 May 1642. This pragmatic step ensured that the children of couples who had married in a civil ceremony were not now deemed to be illegitimate. Nevertheless, the short-lived experiment of operating a civil registration system had failed and it would be some time before a fresh attempt was made.

The next significant act of the restored monarchy, as far as the recording of life events was concerned, related solely to records of burials.

In the decades following the coronation of King Charles II, a succession of related Acts was passed, requiring the dead to be buried in shrouds made from English wool. The initial Act of 1660 was found to be inadequate but later Acts dating from 1678 and 1680 were rather more successful. The main purpose of the Acts was to support the English wool trade and to prevent 'the Exportation of ... Moneyes ... for the buying and importing of Linnen', but there was also a clear potential for raising revenue as a fine of £5 was to be levied against anyone who failed to produce a sworn affidavit that 'burial in woollen' had taken place. Parish registers often have an 'A' or the abbreviation 'Aff.' written next to the burial entries in this period indicating that an affidavit had been produced. Those who were deemed too poor to afford the cost of a woollen shroud were exempted by the Acts but there is strong evidence that non-compliance from anyone else was severely dealt with.

Affidavits start to be recorded in the burial register for Cheshunt, Hertfordshire in August 1678. The entry for Edward Lee's burial on 10 August is annotated with the words 'No Aff[idavi]t. Notice given to Will[ia]m Page, overseer 19 August.'

Refusal to comply wasn't restricted to a particular social class. The Cheshunt registers record the burial of 'Dame Elizabeth, wife of Sir William Glascock' on 10 January 1680/1 and go on to state: 'No Affid[avit]. the penalty paid to the Churchwarden.' Cox quotes two further examples that suggest that 'the higher classes ... regarded it rather as a tax to be paid than a law to be observed' (John Charles Cox, *The Parish Registers of England* (1910), p. 124).

The legislation remained in place until 1814 but was rarely enforced after 1770. However, the registers of Shipston-on-Stour in Worcestershire provide evidence that refusals were still being dealt with as late as 1754, 'Burials. 27 June 1754 – Thomas son of Thomas and Mary BIERLY. NB. No Affidavit being brought within eight Days, Sent a notice of this under my Hand to Mr Hancock & R Rand the Ch. Wardens, dated July 25th – who caused Bierly to comply'. Copies of the affidavits sometimes survive among collections of parochial churchwarden's accounts.

The reign of William and Mary saw the first direct attempts by the Crown to use the registration system as a means of raising revenue. The long-held fears that taxation of the recording of baptisms, marriages and burials would eventually prove too tempting for an impoverished monarch were finally realised in 1695 with the introduction of the 'Act for granting to his Majesty certaine rates and duties upon Marriages Births and Burials'.

This Act was just one of a number of pieces of legislation passed in the late seventeenth century, as William attempted to raise money for the war against France – or, in the words of the Act itself, 'for the necessary defence of your Realmes and the prosecution of a Warr against France with Vigour'.

The idea was that entries in parish registers would be subject to payment of a fee which was dependent on the social standing of the individual or individuals concerned. The basic rate was set at 2s for baptisms, 2s 6d for marriages and 4s for burials, but this could rise to as much as £50 for the marriage or burial of a duke or duchess. Realising that certain sections of the population would easily avoid this tax, the legislation also required an annual payment of 1s to be made by bachelors over 25 years of age and childless widowers.

An amendment to the Act passed in 1696 imposed a fine of 40s on parents who refused to comply, while ministers were liable to the same fine if they failed to record the births of children born in their parish but not baptised in their church. Parents of these children had to pay a fee of 6d to the minister for each child registered.

In many respects, this legislation can be seen as a second attempt to introduce a form of civil registration. At a time when an increasing proportion of the population was attending places of worship outside the established Church of England (and from 1689, people were essentially free to do so) it was important and significant that the Act allowed for the registration of the children of Roman Catholics, Jews, Quakers and other Protestant Nonconformists, and attempted to ensure that they too contributed to the king's war fund.

As with the Parish Registers of the Civil War period, this system was found to be unenforceable and ultimately failed – the Act was repealed in 1706 and the liability to pay any outstanding fines was revoked. However, the tax left behind some remarkable records, offering a tantalising glimpse of what might have been. A document relating to the collection of 'Marriage Tax' payments for the parish of Darley in Derbyshire survives among a collection of records held by Sheffield Archives (Darley 'Marriage Tax', Sheffield Archives, Barker Deeds 728). The document claims to list 'the names degrees titles and qualifications of every person within the Township of Darley' but, of course, this actually means 'every householder', the vast majority being adult males, with a minority of widows and spinsters.

A typical entry from the list reads, 'William Turner his Wife and foure Children'; occupations are occasionally given together with the number of servants in each household; the word 'pentioner' next to an entry indicates that the person was receiving relief from the parish and was therefore exempt from the tax. There were five columns, headed respectively, 'Marriages', 'Births', 'Burialls', 'Bachelors' and 'Widowers', provided to record the payments of the taxes but in the case of the Darley list, only the payments made by bachelors and widowers have been entered.

A fairly comprehensive collection of returns for the City of London also survive and have been indexed and published by the London Record Society as 'London Inhabitants with the Walls, 1695'. The records are available online at http://british-history.ac.uk.

It's clear that the system failed at an early date. The infrastructure required to support an undertaking on this scale was evidently beyond late eighteenth-century English society. Nevertheless, it seems likely that lists would have been created for most parishes and the remarkably small number of surviving lists is therefore quite difficult to explain.

Throughout this period, many rural parishes continued to use a single 'composite' register to record baptisms, marriages and burials, often in separate sections of the register but sometimes entered in a simple chronological run, as the events occurred. Larger parishes generally kept two or three separate registers and for the next fifty years, the parish register system continued in its own quiet way with no significant legislation affecting the recording of our ancestors' vital events.

Then, in 1753, Lord Hardwicke produced his momentous 'Act for the preventing of Clandestine Marriages' – a piece of legislation that, when it became law the following year, fundamentally changed the way in which the whole process of marriage was conducted in England and Wales for the next eighty-three years.

Clandestine marriages had long been a matter of concern, for civil and religious authorities alike. Even before Hardwicke's Act was implemented, marriages (whether by licence or by banns) were supposed to be conducted by an Anglican clergyman in the parish church where one of the parties was resident. The problem was that the 'guidelines' were just that and were entirely unsupported by legislation. Over the years increasing numbers of couples had opted

## Philip Yorke, First Earl of Hardwicke

Philip Yorke was born in Dover on the south coast of England on 1 December 1690. His father, also Philip, was an attorney, while his mother, Elizabeth Gibbon, was related to the historian Edward Gibbon.

The young Philip Yorke was educated by Samuel Morland in Bethnal Green, London and soon demonstrated a strong interest in the law. He was admitted to the Middle Temple on 29 November 1708 and called to the bar on 6 May 1715. During his early years in London, Yorke had made some useful connections, notably Thomas Parker the Lord Chief Justice and he soon became a successful barrister.

On 16 May 1719, at St George's, Hanover Square in Westminster, Philip Yorke married a widow named Margaret Lygon, who was the daughter of a former MP, Charles Cocks. The Cocks family was also well connected: Margaret was the niece of Lord Somers and, through her first marriage, was related to the Master of the Rolls, Sir Joseph Jekylls.

Yorke soon made his fortune. In 1724 he bought the estate of Hardwicke in Gloucestershire and in 1740 he settled with his wife and seven children at Wimpole in Cambridgeshire.

In the same year that he married, Philip Yorke entered Parliament as the MP for Lewes in Sussex and began an illustrious political career. In 1720, aged just 30, he was knighted and was appointed to the role of Solicitor General. He was Attorney General from 1724–33, Chief Justice of the King's Bench from 1733–7 and Lord Chancellor from 1737–56.

In 1733 he was elevated to the peerage as Baron Hardwicke and on 2 April 1754 he was created Viscount Royston and Earl of Hardwicke. It is by this last name that he is best known to history.

As Lord Chancellor, the Earl of Hardwicke was responsible for introducing one of family history's most significant pieces of legislation. Hardwicke's Marriage Act was passed in 1753, coming into force the following year. It was designed to deal with the problem of clandestine marriages by tightening up on procedures and closing a number of loopholes. All marriages would now be conducted according to the rites and ceremonies of the Church of England, either by licence or after the reading of banns, and pages in the marriage registers would be numbered as a measure to prevent fraud.

Jews and Quakers were exempt from the terms of Hardwicke's Act but other Protestant Nonconformists and Roman Catholics were forced to undergo an Anglican ceremony for their marriage to be legally valid.

For family historians, the Act had the effect of standardising marriage entries and ensuring that, in most cases, the parish register is the only place to search for a record of a marriage. The Act remained in force until 1837.

The 1st Earl of Hardwicke died on 6 March 1764 and was buried at Wimpole. He was succeeded by his eldest son Philip (the 2nd Earl of Hardwicke).

Dictionary of National Biography
www.oxforddnb.com/view/article/30245

for a so-called clandestine or irregular marriage, frequently performed by an unbeneficed or defrocked clergyman, and often, but not always, in an area beyond the jurisdiction of the Church of England. The most famous of these was the area around the Fleet Prison in London where as many as 6,000 marriages a year took place during the 1740s.

The attraction of clandestine or irregular marriages was all too obvious: they offered an opportunity for couples to get married without anyone asking too many questions. Some marriages even took place in complete secrecy and unscrupulous clergymen were willing, for a fee, to falsify entries in their registers. And it was this corrupt environment that inspired Lord Hardwicke to draft his great piece of legislation.

For family historians, the most significant part of the Act is the section that stipulates first that 'all Banns of Matrimony shall be published ... in the Parish Church ... In all Cases where Banns shall have been published, the Marriage shall be solemnized in one of the Parish Churches or Chapels where such Banns have been published, and in no other Place whatsoever.' The only other legally valid marriages were by licence and again the rules regarding this process were clearly laid out.

These stringent conditions had the desired effect of closing the clandestine marriage loophole for once and for all. The Act came into effect on 25 March 1754 and between that date and 30 June 1837 all marriages in England and Wales (other than those of Jews and Quakers who were specifically exempted from the terms of Lord Hardwicke's Act) had to take place according to the rites and ceremonies of the established Church of England and had to be solemnised in an Anglican Church or chapel. This meant that Roman Catholics and Protestant Nonconformists were forced to undergo an Anglican ceremony to ensure the legitimacy of their children. It would be wrong to say that marriages performed outside the Church of England during this period were in any way illegal – they simply had no legal status and would not have been recognised by a court of law.

The other main aim of the Act had been to deal with the many problems regarding fraudulent entries in the registers. The practice of making Bishop's Transcripts had gone some way towards dealing with the matter but Hardwicke recognised that the system was far from perfect. The registers used by most parishes were effectively plain notebooks. Marriages were noted on the blank pages, as they occurred, usually with no more information than the date of the marriage and the names of the two parties. Hardwicke recognised that this left the door open for those who might be tempted to falsify entries or even to create entirely fraudulent marriages.

The Act dealt with these 'undue Entries and Abuses in Registers of Marriages' in two ways. All marriages were to be solemnised 'in the Presence of two or more credible Witnesses' and the form of the entries was clearly set out in the Act. But most important of all was the very specific instruction that

the Church-wardens and Chapel-wardens of every Parish or Chapelry shall provide proper Books of Vellum, or good and durable Paper in which all Marriages and Banns of Marriage respectively, there published or solemnized, shall be registered, and every Page thereof shall be marked at the Top, with the Figure of the Number of every such Page, beginning at the second Leaf with Number-one.

*Leeds Parish Register with Hardwicke-style marriage entries from 1754.* (West Yorkshire Archive Service RDP68/4/1)

This was a foolproof way of ensuring that registers could not easily be tampered with.

In practice, most parishes opted to use printed registers but this was not a specific requirement of Hardwicke's Act, which simply insisted that the pages should be numbered. Most parishes also adopted the prudent practice of numbering each of the entries, which provided a further check against potential fraud.

The Act also required parishes to keep records of the calling of banns of marriage, which were usually, but not always, kept in a separate register.

*Chapter 3*

# PARISH REGISTERS, PART 3:
## 'The Imperfect Method . . . Generally Pursued'

Parish registers were now entering the modern era. Coverage (allowing for the not insignificant matter of Nonconformity which will be dealt with in Chapter 7) was as close to comprehensive as could reasonably be expected. But it was becoming clear to many that the system wasn't quite up to the job. The amount of detail recorded in baptismal and burial registers – which, in many cases, still consisted of no more than names and dates – was simply insufficient to allow positive identification of individuals. And in a society with a rapidly growing population and, perhaps more importantly, an increasingly litigious population, the requirement to use parish registers as legal evidence of birth, marriage and death was becoming ever more apparent.

It's true that as the eighteenth century progressed, many parishes had begun to add extra information such as the age at death, or an occupation or place of residence to distinguish two men of the same name. But while this kind of detail went some way towards helping to sort out who was who, for one man it wasn't nearly enough.

The Reverend William Dade held a number of livings in the City of York and the East Riding of Yorkshire during the latter half of the eighteenth century. In 1770, while the minister of St Helen's, York, he outlined a scheme that would put an end to all the uncertainty inherent in what he termed, 'the imperfect method hitherto generally pursued'.

Dade's idea was to record a mass of additional details in the baptismal registers, such as the profession and abode of the father, the names and professions of both sets of grandparents and the child's position in the family (i.e. first son, second son, first daughter, second daughter etc.) as well as their date of birth and baptism. Burial registers would record the deceased's parentage, their age and the cause of death as standard. The overall effect of all of this would be to make identification of individuals for inheritance and other legal purposes relatively straightforward.

Support for Dade's scheme was soon forthcoming and in 1777, the Archbishop of York ordered that 'Dade' registers should be introduced across his diocese. But although a significant number of Yorkshire parishes adopted the system and maintained Dade-style registers for many years, others found that the work involved in collecting and recording the extra information (not to mention the additional effort of copying the entries for the Bishop's Transcripts) was just too great and when the Archbishop announced that failure to use the new format would not be punished, the scheme floundered. Similar registers appeared in other parts of the country including Durham, Cheshire and Wiltshire, but these were generally short-lived and very few continued beyond 1800.

The Dade experiment can be seen as yet another case of 'what might have been'. And unlike the earlier failed schemes, this one didn't even have the advantage of being supported by legislation. Church officials had been asked to operate the scheme without the provision of any additional resources and the amount of detail they were expected to record was far more extensive than the General Register Office expected of its vast army of officials sixty years later, so it's not hard to see why Dade registers were ultimately doomed to failure.

Parish registers were often seen by clergymen as their personal property and they regularly used them to record significant local or national events, such as the death or coronation of a monarch. Some took it upon themselves to make personal comments about their parishioners – most, but by no means all, of a positive nature. The registers of Watlington, Oxfordshire contain a good example of an adult baptism: '1719 29 March, Mr John Stennett, an apothecary of about thirty years old, on Palm Sunday', to which was added in a later hand; 'Became afterwards a villainous Apostate so ought to be erased'.

# William Dade

On 26 January 1740/41, William Dade was baptised at Burton Agnes, near Bridlington in the East Riding of Yorkshire. William was the son of Thomas Dade, the vicar of Burton Agnes, and the entry in the parish register makes interesting reading: 'January 26 William son of the Reverend Mr Thomas Dade Vicar of Agnes Burton'. This is typical of baptismal registers of the time in that his mother's name is not given.

Dade was always destined to follow his father into the Church. He attended schools in Shipton and Holderness in Yorkshire and later at Mr Newcombe's in Hackney, London, all of which was building towards his entry to Cambridge University. On 12 April 1759, he was admitted to St John's College, from where he matriculated at Michaelmas 1762.

He was ordained a deacon on 24 June 1763 and in 1766 became the rector of Barmston, a village situated just a few miles south of Burton Agnes. Dade was to hold the living of Barmston for the rest of his life but he also became the rector of St Mary Castlegate, York, (1773–90), the rector of St Michael-in-Spurriergate, York (1773) and the vicar of Ulrome (1776–90).

In 1783, William Dade became a Fellow of the Society of Antiquaries and this gives a clue to the real passion of his life. At an early age, Dade developed an interest in the history of the Holderness area of the East Riding of Yorkshire.

He spent many years working on his manuscript, an 'Alphabetical Register of Marriages, Births, and Burials of considerable Persons in the County of York', and left behind him an unfinished work, 'The History and Antiquities of Holderness', which was partly published in 1783. The nineteenth-century antiquarian George Poulson based much of his *History and Antiquities of the Seignory of Holderness* (published in 1840) on Dade's research, referring to 'the unpublished manuscripts of the Rev. William Dade'.

But for family historians, Dade is best remembered for his attempt to introduce radical reforms to English parish registers. His research, combined with his first-hand experience as a Church of England vicar, had evidently convinced him that the current system was inadequate. He was presumably also aware of his own uninformative entry in the registers of his father's parish at Burton Agnes.

Dade devised a record-keeping system that he believed would make identification of individuals in the Church of England's parish registers much easier. His campaign was only partly successful; Dade-style registers were introduced in a large number of Yorkshire parishes and spread to other parts of the country where registers either directly or indirectly inspired by Dade were started. Ultimately, however, the task of recording the additional details required by Dade's improved parish registers proved too much for the Church of England and by the start of the nineteenth century there were very few Dade-style registers still in operation.

William Dade never married and died after a short illness on 2 August 1790 in the Rectory at Barmston aged just 50.

Dictionary of National Biography
www.oxforddnb.com/view/article/6998

Others mentioned outbreaks of disease that might have a direct impact on the numbers of entries made in their registers. William Bellamy, the curate of Shipston-on-Stour, commented at the end of the burial entries for 1756 that 'a Putrid Fever raged in the Town this year of w[hi]ch about 40 Persons died'.

The rise of Potestant Nonconformity and the resurgence of Roman Catholicism in the late eighteenth century presented fresh challenges for the ecclesiastical authorities, who were, after all, supposed to be providing a general registration system and not just recording the baptisms and burials of their own parishioners. While the vast majority appear to have ignored this aspect of their job, it's clear that some ministers took the role very seriously. An entry in the parish registers of Allhallows, Barking by the Tower, in the City of London, dating from 1793, records the births of Jane and William, the children of John and Ann Thomson. The clerk notes that, 'The above two Entries are made at the request of the Parents of the above mentioned Children in order that they may ascertain legally the place of their respective Births, their parents being of the Persuasion of the People call'd quakers, and as such, these Children have not been baptiz'd by the Minister.'

A decade earlier, in June 1783, the births of David and Baerent, the sons of Reuben and Hannah Solomons, are recorded in the same register. This time the clerk explains that. 'These above entries are made at the request and on the information of their Father, who imagining it may be of service to the above two Children hereafter, though not Baptized here (as being Jews) to know the place of their Birth.'

Examples of this phenomenon are admittedly rare but they serve as a reminder that records of birth are not always found in expected places and that prior to the introduction of civil registration in 1837, the Church of England's parish registers constituted the only official, legally valid means of recording births, marriages and deaths.

And the challenge of providing a comprehensive registration service was made all the harder with the introduction of a stamp duty on parish register entries on 1 October 1783. Presumably having learnt lessons from the unsuccessful attempt to raise a similar tax in the previous century, the stamp duty was a much simpler affair. A flat rate of 3*d* was raised on every entry in the register and the payments were to be made directly to the clergy. This cast the Church in the unfamiliar and unwelcome role of tax collector.

The establishment of a flat rate may have simplified the adminis-tration and collection of the stamp duty but it was this very concept that led to its being seen as a deeply unfair tax, costing the poor as much as it did the rich. Cox, in *The Parish Registers of England* (1910, p. 11), describes it as an 'unpopular and obnoxious statute' and its unpopularity, combined with a lack of support from the clergy which was perhaps understandable given the circumstances, meant that it was always doomed to failure. The Act was repealed in 1794 and it proved to be the last occasion on which the authorities attempted to use registration of life events as an explicit means of raising revenue.

The Act required that Churchwardens and Overseers should pro-vide registers to record the 'burials, marriages, births and christenings' (in most cases these would be the existing parish registers) and required the same parish officials to allow the registers to be inspected by the Commissioners of Stamp Duties and to 'pay unto the Receiver General for the time being … all such Sum and Sums of Money which …

ought to be paid in respect of all and every such Entry and Entries as shall be written in such Register'.

Burials from the workhouse were exempt from the charge, as were the christenings of children whose parents were in receipt of poor relief. For this reason, it is common to see the words 'poor' or 'pauper' written next to parish register entries at this period. Notes about the collection of the duty are also frequently recorded. The baptismal register for St Mary's, Islington, for example, includes the following note at the end of the entries for 1783, 'Inspected & Duty received to the Thirty first December 1783. B Keene In[s]p[ecto]ʳ'.

On 2 October 1783, the register for Great Stanmore records the introduction of 'the Tax for Marriages Births Christenings and Burials' and from this date, the number '3' or sometimes '3d' is written after every entry where the duty was payable. This simple method was evidently used by the inspectors and the parish officials to calculate the amount of duty payable.

As the nineteenth century approached the practice of recording ages in burial registers became more and more common, but it was far from being universal and it was to take a major piece of legislation to change things for the better.

George Rose had first-hand experience of the shortcomings of the parish register system. In a speech to Parliament in February 1812 he described the 'slovenly manner' in which many registers were kept and spoke of how 'he had found, as Treasurer of the Navy, number-less instances of the widows of seamen, who, from this culpable negligence, were not able to prove their marriages'. There was also increasing concern from those sections of society where proving descent for legal purposes was of paramount importance about the deficiencies of the current system. A letter appeared in the *Gentleman's Magazine* in March 1812 referring to Rose's proposed Bill. The writer expressed a commonly held view: 'There cannot be a doubt that in a country where the descent of real and personal property is governed by established rules of legal consanguinity, the faithful preservation of records of baptisms, marriages and burials, ought to be held as an object of the highest importance ...'. As an example of the poor state of affairs, the writer describes how he found the register of the parish of Kelsterne, Lincolnshire in the possession of the rector of Weldon in Northamptonshire – some 80 miles away.

It was Rose's intention to introduce a Bill 'to enact that all registers throughout the kingdom should be uniform' and at the same time to improve the conditions in which the registers were kept. He also wanted to give Nonconformists the right to deliver copies of their registers to the 'clergyman of the established church' so that they could be given equal legal standing with those of the Church of England. The Parish Registers' Bill that went to the House of Lords made frequent references to registers of *'births'* but the Act that was eventually passed contained no such references (despite the word appearing in the title of the Act): all mention of Nonconformists had also disappeared.

Nonetheless, Rose's 'Act for the better regulating and preserving Parish and other Registers of Births, Baptisms, Marriages, and Burials, in England' was a significant piece of legislation. From 1813, all parish registers were to be standardised, ensuring that certain pieces of information were consistently recorded throughout England and Wales. The amount of detail fell somewhat short of what William Dade had proposed some thirty-five years earlier, but it still represented an improvement on what had gone before. Disappointingly, there was no place for mothers' maiden names in the baptismal registers, or for any parental details on marriage entries. There was even at least one retrograde step: the burial registers allowed no space to record the deceased's occupation or their marital status – details that had frequently appeared in pre-Rose registers.

George Rose's ambitious scheme to establish an effective registry of births, marriages and deaths had been watered down by the more conservative elements in Parliament, and many of his concerns about the deficiencies of the current system had not been fully addressed. And it was these concerns that would ultimately lead to the establishment of a civil registration system.

The format for the Church of England's baptismal and burial registers, introduced by Rose's Act, is still in force today, and although they are no longer used for most legal purposes, they continue to be kept to this day. Rose-style registers were also adopted by a number of Nonconformist congregations and were used by an assortment of

**1044**   **C. 145, 146.**   **52° GEORGII III.**   **A.D.1812.**

liable to the fame Toll, and no more, as the fame would have been if paffing through the faid Gate drawn by One Horfe only ; and where any Horfe fhall be faftened to but not ufed in drawing any Waggon, Cart or other Carriage, fuch Horfe fhall not be liable to a higher Toll than a fingle Horfe ; provided, that if any Coach, Chariot, Chaife, Chair, Cart or other Carriage, fo affixed, tied or fecured to any Waggon or Cart, fhall have any Goods conveyed therein, other than the Harnefs thereof, and fuch Articles of Package as may be neceffary for the Protection of fuch Carriages, the fame fhall be liable to Double the Toll hereby impofed.

*Public Act.* VIII. And be it further enacted, That this Act fhall be deemed and taken to be a Public Act, and fhall be judicially taken Notice of as fuch by all Judges, Juftices and others, without being fpecially pleaded.

### C A P. CXLVI.

An Act for the better regulating and preferving Parifh and other Regifters of Births, Baptifms, Marriages and Burials in *England*.   [28th *July* 1812.]

'WHEREAS the amending the Manner and Form of keeping and of preferving Regifters of Baptifms, 'Marriages and Burials, of His Majefty's Subjects in the feveral Parifhes and Places in *England*, will 'greatly facilitate the Proof of Pedigrees of Perfons claiming to be entitled to Real or Perfonal Eftates, and 'be otherwife of great public Benefit and Advantage ;' Be it therefore enacted by the King's Moft Excellent Majefty, by and with the Advice and Confent of the Lords Spiritual and Temporal, and Commons, in this pre-

*Officiating Mi-*
*nifters to keep*
*Regifters of Pub-*
*lic and Private*
*Baptifms of*
*Marriages and*
*of Burials.*
*Parifhes to pro-*
*vide fuitable*
*Books for that*
*Purpofe.*
fent Parliament affembled, and by the Authority of the fame, That, from and after the Thirty firft Day of *December* One thoufand eight hundred and twelve, Regifters of Public and Private Baptifms, Marriages and Burials, folemnized according to the Rites of the United Church of *England* and *Ireland*, within all Parifhes or Chapelries in *England*, whether fubject to the Ordinary or Peculiar, or other Jurifdiction, fhall be made and kept by the Rector, Vicar, Curate or Officiating Minifter of every Parifh, (or of any Chapelry where the Ceremonies of Baptifm, Marriage and Burial have been ufually and may according to Law be performed) for the time being, in Books of Parchment, or of good and durable Paper, to be provided by His Majefty's Printer as Occafion may require, at the Expence of the refpective Parifhes or Chapelries ; whereon fhall be printed, upon each Side of every Leaf, the Heads of Information herein required to be entered in the Regifters of Baptifms, Marriages and Burials refpectively, and every fuch Entry fhall be numbered progreffively from the Beginning to the End of each Book, the Firft Entry to be diftinguifhed by Number One ; and every fuch Entry fhall be divided from the Entry next following by a printed Line, according to the Forms contained in the Schedules (A.) (B.) (C.) hereto annexed ; and every Page of every fuch Book fhall be numbered with progreffive Numbers, the firft Page being marked with the Number t. in the Middle of the upper Part of fuch Page, and every fubfequent Page being marked in like manner with progreffive Numbers, from Number 1. to the End of the Book.

*King's Printer to*
*tranfmit to each*
*Parifh a printed*
*Copy of Act,*
*and Regifter*
*Books adapted*
*to Forms*
*prefcribed.*
II. And, for better enfuring the Regularity and Uniformity of fuch Regifter Books, be it further enacted, That a printed Copy of this Act, together with one Book fo prepared as aforefaid, and adapted to the Form of the Regifter of Baptifms prefcribed in the Schedule (A.) to this Act annexed ; and alfo one other Book fo prepared as aforefaid, and adapted to the Form prefcribed for the Regifter of Marriages in the Schedule (B.) to this Act annexed ; and alfo one other Book fo prepared as aforefaid, and adapted to the Form prefcribed for the Regifter of Burials in the Schedule (C.) to this Act annexed, fhall, as foon as conveniently may be after the paffing of this Act, be provided and tranfmitted by His Majefty's Printer to the Officiating Minifters of the feveral Parifhes and Chapelries in *England* refpectively, who are hereby required to ufe and apply the fame in and to the Purpofes of this Act ; and fuch Books refpectively fhall be proportioned to the Population of the feveral Parifhes and Chapelries, according to the laft Returns of fuch Population made under the Authority of Parliament ; and other Books of like Form and Quality fhall for the like Purpofes be furnifhed from time to time by the Churchwardens or Chapelwardens of every Parifh or Chapelry, at the Expence of the faid Parifh or Chapelry, whenever they fhall be required by the Rector, Vicar, Curate or Officiating Minifter to provide the fame ; and all fuch Books fhall be of Paper, unlefs required to be of Parchment by fuch Churchwardens or Chapelwardens refpectively.

*Regifters in*
*feparate Regifter*
*Books.*
III. And be it further enacted, That fuch Regifters fhall be kept in fuch feparate Books aforefaid, and that every fuch Rector, Vicar, Curate or Officiating Minifter fhall as foon as poffible after the Solemnization of every Baptifm, whether Private or Public, or Burial refpectively, record and enter in a fair and legible Handwriting, in the proper Regifter Book to be provided, made and kept as aforefaid, the feveral Particulars defcribed in the feveral Schedules hereinbefore mentioned, and fign the fame ; and in no cafe, unlefs prevented by Sicknefs, or other unavoidable Impediment, later than within Seven Days after the Ceremony of any fuch Baptifm or Burial fhall have taken place.

*Certificate of*
*Baptifm, &c.*
*when performed*
*in other Place*
*than Parifh*
*Church, &c.*
*according to*
*Schedule (D)*
*Entry of Bap-*
*tifm, &c.*
*diftinguifhed*
*accordingly.*
IV. And be it further enacted, That whenever the Ceremony of Baptifm or Burial fhall be performed in any other Place than the Parifh Church or Church Yard of any Parifh (or the Chapel or Chapel Yard of any Chapelry, providing its own diftinct Regifters) and fuch Ceremony fhall be performed by any Minifter not being the Rector, Vicar, Minifter or Curate of fuch Parifh or Chapelry, the Minifter who fhall perform fuch Ceremony of Baptifm or Burial fhall, on the fame or on the next Day, tranfmit to the Rector, Vicar or other Minifter of fuch Parifh or Chapelry, or his Curate, a Certificate of fuch Baptifm or Burial in the Form contained in the Schedule (D.) to this Act annexed, and the Rector, Vicar, Minifter or Curate of fuch Parifh or Chapelry, fhall thereupon enter fuch Baptifm or Burial according to fuch Certificate in the Book kept purfuant to this Act for fuch Purpofe ; and fhall add to fuch Entry the following Words, " According to the " Certificate of the Reverend            tranfmitted to me on the            Day " of          ."

V. And

*Rose's 'Act for better regulating and preserving Parish and other Registers of Births, Baptisms, Marriages and Burials, in England', 1812.*

## George Rose

George Rose was born on 17 January 1744 in the Forfarshire parish of Stracartho, the son of David Rose and his wife Margaret (née Rose). His father was an Episcopalian minister who, the year following George's birth, was caught up in the Jacobite uprising. George was sent to London where he was brought up by an uncle and educated at Westminster School. In 1758 he joined the Royal Navy as a midshipman on the *Infernal* and he served throughout the Seven Years War before being discharged in 1762.

After leaving the Navy, Rose found work as a clerk and was involved in publishing the *Journal of the House of Lords*. This work brought him into contact with some influential people; in particular Lord Sandwich and Hugh Hume, the Earl of Marchmont.

On 7 July 1769 at St George's, Hanover Square, George Rose married Theodora Duer, the daughter of a wealthy West Indian plantation owner, Major John Duer. George and Theodora had three children: George Henry (ca.1770–1855), Frances Theodora (ca.1771–1846) and William Stewart (ca.1775–1843).

Rose entered Parliament in 1784. He was the MP for Launceston from 1784–8, Lymington from 1788–90 and Christchurch from 1790–1818. He became a close friend of Pitt's government. In 1788 he was appointed Clerk to the Parliaments, a position he held for thirty years. He also held the posts of Secretary to the Treasury, Vice-President of the Board of Trade, Paymaster of the Forces, and, most significantly, Treasurer of the Navy from 1807–18. It was his experience in this last role that convinced him that the state of the country's parish registers was a matter that needed to be addressed.

In 1812, George Rose introduced his Parish Registers' Bill into Parliament. It was passed by both houses with some major amendments and, as *An Act for the better regulating and preserving Parish and other Registers of Births, Baptisms, Marriages, and Burials, in England*, became law on 28 June 1812. The Act came into force on 1 January 1813.

Although of great significance to family historians, the Act represented just one of many causes in which Rose became interested during his long and distinguished career. He was an active parliamentarian who never shied from controversy and held strong views on many of the major issues of the day, including Roman Catholicism, parliamentary reform and the abolition of slavery. Rose continued to campaign right into his final years and as late as 1817 he was at the forefront of the movement to promote savings banks. He also served as a trustee of the British Museum, an elder of Trinity House and a director of the Royal Naval Hospital at Greenwich.

In 1784 George Rose had bought the Hampshire estate of Cuffnells. He spent a large sum of money making improvements to the old house and died there on 13 January 1818. He is buried in the family vault in Christ Church Priory Church along with his wife Theodora (who survived him until 1834) and two of her spinster sisters.

Dictionary of National Biography
www.oxforddnb.com/view/article/24088

non-parochial institutions such as workhouses, hospitals and army barracks.

During the nineteenth century the country underwent a dramatic change, from a society that was largely rural to one that was predominantly urban. One of the side effects of this transformation was that the inner city churches began to struggle to deal with their ever growing congregations – both living and dead. The answer for the living was to carve new smaller ecclesiastical districts out of the existing ancient parishes – an extensive building campaign took place in the 1820s and 1830s providing hundreds of new churches in towns and cities around the country. But the land required for new churchyards with burial plots was simply not available in the densely populated urban areas and the problem of what to do with the bodies of the deceased became an increasing concern, particularly in London.

In 1832, Parliament passed a statute authorising the creation of seven private cemeteries, to be located all around the edge of the city. The opening of Kensal Green Cemetery (in 1832), West Norwood (1837), Highgate (1839), Abney Park (1840), Nunhead (1840), Brompton (1840) and Tower Hamlets (1841) went some way to alleviating the problem of London's overcrowded churchyards. However, it wasn't until Brookwood Cemetery was opened in 1854, served by its own railway line and with enough room to cope with the needs of London's

BURIALS in the Parish of _Stepney Trinity District_ in the County of _Middlesex_ in the Year 1849

| Name. | Abode. | When buried. | Age. | By whom the Ceremony was performed. |
|---|---|---|---|---|
| 1849 | | | | |
| No. 97 Samuel Miller | 9 Canal Rd Mile End | Nov 14 | 42 | James Rumfield |
| No. 98 Ship[?] Waters | 21 Coburn Rd Bow | Feb 11 | 80 | E. J. Fuller |
| No. 99 James Williamson | Kingston Cottg Coburn Road Bow | Feb 19 | 58 | Henry Badak |
| No. 100 Mary Thurman | 10 Aberfield Square Old Ford | April 1st | 70 | James Rumfield Off. Pfm |
| No. 101 Bridget Onslow | 32 Coburn Strt Bow | April 19 | 79 | James Rumfield off. Min |
| No. 102 David Waters | 35 Trafalgar Square Bow | April 29 | 63 | James Rumford off. Min |
| No. 103 Margaret Laura Pashly | 16 Gove Road | June 23 | 1 | Henry Randall |
| No. 104 Thomas Onslow | 34 Coburn Street Bow | Aug 4 | 70 | James Rumford Curate |

BURIALS in the Parish of _Stepney Trinity District_ in the County of _Middlesex_ in the Year 1847–8

| Name. | Abode. | When buried. | Age. | By whom the Ceremony was performed. |
|---|---|---|---|---|
| No. 89 Sarah Braddon | 3 Hope Place Grove Street Mile End | April 10 | 57 | James Rumford Curate |
| No. 90 Mary Faygenbothan | Grove Street Mile End | July 29 | 51 | Edward Boyle |
| No. 91 Mary Lillies | 48 Charlotte Stret Mile End Cecilia | 79 | James Rumford Curate |
| No. 92 Sara L Braxton | Cross Avenue Mile End | May 5 1848 | 78 | Henry Bodell m.a. Incumbent |
| No. 93 Frederick Hempall | Upper Clapton Hackney | May 25 | 19 | Henry Randall |
| No. 94 Arthur Rickets | 17 Regent St | July 10 | 18 | Henry Randall |
| No. 95 Mary Ann Ferril | 40 Trafalgar Sq | October 2 | 87 | James Rumford Curate |
| No. 96 Maria Roses Martins | 17 College Gove | Oct 24 | 42 | Henry Lendall |

Mile End Holy Trinity Parish Register with Rose-style burial entries from 1847–9. (London Metropolitan Archives P73/TRI/28) dead for 500 years, that the problem was finally solved. At around the same time that Brookwood Cemetery was opened, Parliament took the decision to close the old inner city churchyards to new burials.

All of these multi-denominational cemeteries kept their own burial records, using Rose-style registers, as did the large numbers of municipal cemeteries that had sprung up around the country in the latter half of the nineteenth century.

Some parishes bought land on the outskirts of London, often many miles from the mother church, and established new cemeteries for the benefit of their parishioners: Islington, St Pancras and Marylebone cemeteries are in East Finchley, Paddington in Willesden and Mill Hill, while the City of Westminster Cemetery was rather confusingly located in Hanwell, in rural west Middlesex.

The Church of England had held the role of official state registrar for nearly 300 years but the early decades of the nineteenth century saw increasing dissatisfaction with the parish register system: it was time for the civil authorities to take over.

*Chapter 4*

# CIVIL REGISTRATION, PART 1:
## 'A Complete Register of the Births, Deaths and Marriages of His Majesty's Subjects in England'

Civil registration of births, marriages and deaths in England and Wales began on 1 July 1837. Although it is a date that looms large among family historians, it was not regarded by most people at the time as the biggest event of the year. King William IV had died less than two weeks earlier, and had been succeeded by the young Queen Victoria; and voting began in a general election later the same month. The general election resulted in a fourth successive victory for the Whigs, and it was their dominance of government since the Reform Act of 1832 that had finally led to the establishment of civil registration after many failed attempts. The Act for Registering Births, Deaths and Marriages in England 1836 finally passed into law, after many amendments. It provided for the establishment of a General Register Office in London, and the appointment of a Registrar General to run it.

The registration of life events in the registers of the Church of England had long been known to be defective, and was partially remedied by Lord Hardwicke's Act of 1753 to regulate marriages, and by Rose's Act of 1812 for baptisms and burials. But those reforms had done nothing to address the problems of registration of the births, marriages and deaths of non-Anglicans, who were increasing in number. Because of its position as the Established Church of England and Wales, the registers of the Church of England had a legal status denied to those of any other denomination, regardless of the quality of their record keeping. This had become increasingly unpopular with the various Protestant Nonconformist congregations and Roman Catholics, who had, since 1754, been required to marry according to the rites of the Church of England for their marriages to be valid, and for their children to be legitimate in the eyes of the law. Similarly, a Church of England baptism certificate constituted legal proof of age and of parentage, so committed Nonconformists might find it expedient to baptise their children into a church the beliefs of which they did not share, for entirely legal reasons. Only in death could they escape the clutches of the Established Church, and even then only if there was a burial ground for their chosen denomination in the vicinity.

Having an effective monopoly in the business of legal registration was of course very good news for the Church of England. However much the clergy might bemoan decreasing congregations, enticed away by charismatic preachers, or more attractive forms of service elsewhere, they could rest secure in the knowledge that they had a captive audience for marriages and, to a certain extent, baptisms; and, of course, the guaranteed income that went with it. When it was suggested that a neutral, non-denominational form of registration might be introduced, the Church strongly opposed it. Some objections were made on moral and spiritual grounds, no doubt sincerely held, but there is no denying that fears of the effect on the Church's future income were also very real.

The two main parliamentary parties were divided on religious lines, the Tories being identified with the Established Church, and the Whigs with Protestant Nonconformity. Political arguments were often expressed in religious terms, and each side criticised the vested interests of the other. There were several attempts to introduce some kind of civil registration system in the 1820s, none of them successful. This was partly due to the failure of the various Nonconformist churches to present a united front; they all agreed that the current arrangements were unsatisfactory, but could not agree on how best to replace them. Another reason was that any new Bill had to be passed by both the Lords and the Commons before passing into law, and could be amended by either chamber. A Bill could not be sent back and forth indefinitely, however, and if it was not passed at the third attempt it was lost altogether, and its proposers would have to start again. The Tory majority in the Lords made a number of amendments to the 1836 Bill before sending it for its final reading in the Commons, which is why the 1836 Registration Acts were so flawed, but the government was reluctant to lose yet another attempt at reform, so the Acts were passed, with the intention of amending them later. In the event it was to be almost four decades before this was done.

In the meantime, the General Register Office was able to open for business and do the best it could with the imperfect legislation. It was a start. For the population at large this momentous event largely passed unnoticed. Unless someone in your immediate family married, had a baby or died, new regulations about registering these events would have no impact at all. Most couples who were about to marry did exactly what they would have done a year or a decade earlier; they had the banns called in the parish church, and they married there. The only difference was that more information about them would be written in the registers that they signed. Very few people took advantage of the facility to marry in a Nonconformist church or chapel to start with, and even fewer chose to be married by a registrar in an entirely secular ceremony.

In order to administer this new system, the country needed to be divided into manageable units, and the General Register Office took advantage of the recently created Poor Law Unions set up in 1834 to do this. The unions were, for the most part, created by uniting groups of adjacent parishes into larger units, which were judged to be suitable units on which to base the new registration districts, with the added advantage of a ready-made workforce who could take on registration duties in addition to their existing jobs. As a result, the Poor Law and registration systems were inextricably bound together for many years to come. The terms '(Poor Law) Union' and 'registration district' are therefore almost synonymous in the nineteenth and early twentieth centuries; almost, but not quite. Theory was quickly overtaken by practicality, and some smaller unions were annexed to adjacent larger ones for registration purposes. The shortest-lived registration districts were Hursley, joined to Winchester, Sedgefield to Stockton, Lanchester to Durham and Whitchurch to Wem, all within three months of the start of registration in 1837. Lanchester and

*Somerset House, the home of the General Register Office from its inception in 1837.* (Charles Knight, *London,* n.d.)

Whitchurch re-emerged as districts in their own right, in 1875 and 1853 respectively. A dozen more amalgamations took place before the 1830s were out. But three years after the Poor Law Act, unions had still not been formed in parts of Lancashire and Yorkshire, where there was vigorous local opposition to the new arrangements for poor relief, so temporary 'unions' were imposed for registration purposes while negotiations continued.

A registration district was divided into sub-districts, each of which was made up of several parishes, or sometimes just one. Some smaller registration districts only had a single sub-district, and there was considerable variation in the area and population of districts and sub-districts throughout the country. This was the inevitable result of trying to make an administrative framework cope with populations as diverse as densely populated city centres and remote rural areas, with all the variations in between. A Superintendent Registrar was in charge of each registration district, and this post was offered to the Clerk to the Board of Guardians for that Union. Almost all of them accepted, and the few who did not were generally close to retirement and therefore unwilling to take on extra areas of responsibility for a short time. A Registrar of Births and Deaths was appointed for each sub-district, and a Registrar of Marriages who could register marriages throughout the whole district. Most districts had only one marriage registrar in the early years. Registrars were not salaried, but were paid on 'piece work' according to the number of events they registered. Most combined their registration duties with other jobs, although in some urban areas there might be enough births and deaths for a man to make a living from registration work alone. Many of the first registrars were medical men or Poor Law Union officials, primarily Relieving Officers, who were well placed to combine registration duties with their existing occupations. Superintendent Registrars, who were also Clerks to the Guardians, were usually solicitors or attorneys.

Registrars did not have the easiest of jobs in the early years of registration. First of all they had to introduce a new and untried system to a population that was often suspicious, and sometimes hostile. There was widespread publicity about the new rules, and on the whole people complied with them, but there were pockets of active resistance. A number of registrars complained to the Registrar General about people who refused to register the births of their children, claiming that a baptism in the Church of England was sufficient. Others would supply the information, but refused to sign the register. In some places the opposition was organised by the local clergyman and some registrars complained of great difficulty in persuading parents to register births in individual parishes within their districts. The Reverend Boyle of Wolverhampton was particularly vociferous in his opposition, and actively encouraged his parishioners to refuse to co-operate with the registration authorities. As an ordained minister of the Church of England he performed many marriage ceremonies, and he was equally obstructive with regard to these registers, and only handed over his completed registers to the Superintendent Register after several reminders. He was not the only clergyman to object to the new registration laws, but he was probably the most troublesome. Most clergy, however, were perfectly co-operative, and some of them even became registrars of births and deaths.

There was less opposition to the new requirement to register deaths, although a small number of coroners refused to sign death registers, as they were required to do under the Act, claiming that it was not part of their duties. The law now also required that if a death certificate was not produced before a burial took place, then the officiating minister should immediately notify the registrar of births and deaths. This was not always complied with in the early years, but in general the rate of registration of deaths was significantly higher than for births.

More information was recorded in the civil registers of birth, marriage and death than in the equivalent Church of England baptism, marriage and burial registers, which is clearly of great benefit to family historians. But it might have been even better: there had been a number of different proposals in the 1820s and 1830s, including a suggestion to include details of the parents' marriage on a birth certificate. On death registrations, the cause of death was added only at a very late stage to please the medical community.

The formats arrived at in 1837 were to remain unchanged until 1969. A birth record showed the date and place of birth, the sex of the child, and a name if the parents had chosen one. The time of birth was given only for multiple births, but in the 1830s and early 1840s some registrars appeared to be in the habit of recording the time of all births. The early instructions to registrars contained examples of completed entries, including one showing the time of birth, so the registrars getting to grips with their new duties may have taken this to mean that they should always record this information. The place of birth might be an exact address, but in rural areas can just be the name of a village or hamlet. If the parents had not decided on a name by the time they registered the birth, it could be added later on at the time of baptism, and there was a column on the right-hand side of

# CERTIFIED COPY OF AN ENTRY OF BIRTH

GIVEN AT THE **GENERAL REGISTER OFFICE**

*Application Number* 1399124-1

## ST. GILES CAMBERWELL

REGISTRATION DISTRICT

1838 BIRTH in the Sub-district of **Saint Georges, Camberwell** in the County of Surrey

| Columns:- | 1 | 2 | 3 | 4 | 5 | 6 | 7 | 8 | 9 | 10 |
|---|---|---|---|---|---|---|---|---|---|---|
| No. | When and where born | Name, if any | Sex | Name and surname of father | Name, surname and maiden surname of mother | Occupation of father | Signature, description and residence of informant | When registered | Signature of registrar | Name entered after registration |
| 195 | Twenty Fifth July 1838. at No. 2, James Buildings Thomas Street. | Edward | boy | Samuel Tuffen. | Mary Ann Tuffen, formerly Bushby. | Fishmonger | Mary Ann Tuffen her × mark for Tuffen Mother No. 2 James Buildings Thomas Street. | Twentieth of August 1838. | William Wilson Registrar | |

CERTIFIED to be a true copy of an entry in the certified copy of a Register of Births in the District above mentioned.

Given at the GENERAL REGISTER OFFICE, under the Seal of the said Office, the 10th day of July 2009

**BXCD 979968**

1013256 16848 11/08 IMMPSL 024428

*Birth certificate of Edward Tuffen, 1838.* (General Register Office Q3 1838, Camberwell IV 156)

the form for this purpose. However, a fee was payable for this service, and it was very rarely used. The great majority of registrations without a name are for children who died so soon after birth that they were never named at all. The names of both parents are shown, and these are usually those of a married couple, in the form of 'John Smith [and] Mary Smith, formerly Brown'. If the woman had been married before, she would appear as 'Mary Smith, late Jones, formerly Brown'. Unmarried parents would be shown as 'John Smith [and] Mary Brown'. In most cases of births to unmarried parents, however, the father's name simply does not appear at all. This can make it much harder to trace the family further back, but it is not always the end of the line. Sometimes there is a clue to the father's identity in the child's name; if there is a surname for a middle name, there is a good chance that this is the father's surname. Just occasionally the father's full name will be added to the child's, which is a very strong hint indeed. The father's occupation is given next, and then the signature and address of the informant, who is almost always one of the parents, and the address is usually the same as the place of birth. If the address is different it may mean that the family had moved since the birth, but it is more likely that the birth took place away from the family home; for example a young wife might return to her parents' home for the birth of her first child.

A birth had to be registered by one of the parents, or by a 'qualified informant', within forty-two days; if they left it any longer they could still register the birth, but had to pay a fine. Late registrations required the signature of the Superintendent Registrar as well as that of the registrar of births. Some tardy parents saved themselves this expense by simply giving the registrar a date of birth that was within the time limit. If the child had been baptised very soon after birth they might go through life with certificates that seem to suggest they had been baptised while still in the womb! Since the registrar was paid by results, he had every incentive to seek out the parents of newborns, and was likely to call on them at home with his register to facilitate this. Some even employed agents on commission to keep them informed of births they might otherwise miss if their district was a large one.

Marriage entries are worth close attention, because they contain a great deal of useful information, but they should not always be taken at face value. Most marriages ceremonies were still in the Church of England, as before, with small numbers conducted according to Jewish or Quaker rites, these two groups retaining the exemptions they had been granted by Hardwicke's Marriage Act. The only new marriages were those performed by registrars, mainly in Nonconformist churches and chapels. The register books for the different types of marriage ceremony were similar, but not identical. Each entry was headed with the place of marriage; Church of England registers were pre-printed with the wording 'According to the rites and ceremonies of the Church of England' and the registrars' books read 'According to the rites and ceremonies of ...' with a blank space where the denomination of the chapel was inserted. It was also stated whether the marriage was after banns, by registrar's certificate or by licence. Banns and ecclesiastical licences for marriages were administered by the Church of England, exactly as before, but marriage by registrar's certificate was new.

A couple wishing to marry now had the option of giving notice to the Superintendent Registrar three weeks before their intended date of marriage. This was the equivalent of Church of England banns, and was intended to be the preliminary to any kind of marriage, but in practice was used for marriages in Nonconformist chapels or register offices. The date of the marriage was shown, followed by the full names and ages of both parties. Ages might only be indicated as 'full' or 'minor', meaning 21 and upwards or under 21, respectively. This was the age at which people could marry without parental consent, until 1970. The occupations and current addresses of the bride and groom were recorded, followed by the names of their fathers, and the fathers' occupations. The register entry was then signed by both parties, at least two witnesses and the officiating clergyman or registrar.

Ages on marriage certificates are often inaccurate, either because people did not know their exact ages, or else they gave false ages. This might be to minimise a large age gap between bride and groom, but is more often people claiming to be 21 when they were in fact under age. Registrars and clergy were not required to ask for documentary proof of age. Fathers' occupations are often adjusted to make them appear higher up the social scale, and parties may not use exactly the names they were given at birth; giving notice or having the banns called required the names by which they were known at the time, so if they were brought up by a stepfather, that is the surname they are likely to use.

A marriage certificate obtained from the General Register Office is supposedly identical to the original register entry, but you should look at the original register if you can. Errors can occur during the copying process, and the original entry will also have genuine signatures – if the parties were able to sign their names. The Church of England registers have mostly been deposited in county record offices; many have also been filmed and increasing numbers are online. Access to other marriage registers may be more difficult, and the only record of a register office marriage will be held in the register office, where it is not permitted to browse the registers. Some of the errors in the quarterly returns that make up the General Register Office marriage registers are minor, such as small variations in the spelling of a name or a place, but others are more serious. For example, in 1856 Joseph Rhodes married Sarah Ridgway in the parish church in Stockport, Cheshire. This is correctly recorded in the original church register and in the copy held in the register office in Stockport. However, you will not find this marriage in the General Register Office, where the quarterly returns and the index list the groom as John Rhodes, not Joseph.

Death certificates contain disappointingly little information, compared to those of many other countries (including Scotland). They give the date and place of death, the name and age of the deceased, the cause of death and the signature and address of the informant, who may be a relative. The death entry for a child will usually give the name of the father, and that of a married woman or a widow will usually show the name of her husband. The entry for an adult unmarried woman might even show the name of her father, but not necessarily. A sudden death might be the subject of a coroner's inquest, in which case the coroner would be the informant. Although the cause of death appears to have been included on death certificates to placate the medical establishment, actual medical certification of death was not required in this period. You will therefore see such un-medical descriptions as 'act of god' or 'old age'.

## Chapter 5

# CIVIL REGISTRATION, PART 2:
## 'It is Expedient to Amend the Acts Relating to the Registration of Births and Deaths in England'

W hen the 1836 Acts came into force, they were acknowledged to be imperfect. The priority had been to get a system of civil registration up and running after several failed attempts, and the imperfections could be sorted out later. In the event, this took nearly four decades. The 1874 Act for the registering of Births, Deaths, and Marriages made a number of significant and much-needed changes, and came into force in 1875. What it did NOT do, however, was make any difference to the rate of birth registration.

You will often come across statements to the effect that registration was not compulsory before 1875, the implication being that if you cannot find a birth entry before this date, the birth probably wasn't registered. This sounds quite plausible, but there is absolutely no evidence to support it, and quite a lot to disprove it. The phrase in the 1836 Act, 'That the Father or Mother of any Child ... may, within Forty-two Days next after the Day of such Birth ... give Notice of such Birth or Death to the Registrar of the District', is often cited as evidence that registration was optional, but the act goes on to state 'That the Father or Mother of every child ... shall, within Forty-two Days next after the Day of every such Birth, give Information, upon being requested so to do, to the said Registrar'.

So parents could be prosecuted for failing to provide information or to sign the birth register, and a number of them were. The wording of the new Act now clearly made it the responsibility of the parents, rather than the registrar, to ensure that the birth was registered. In practice, the overall rate of non-registration for the whole period from 1837 was estimated to be no more than about 7 per cent, and had steadily decreased since the introduction of registration. Even in the early years studies have shown that the areas where births went unregistered tended to be concentrated in crowded inner cities and in remote areas such as Cornwall and mid-Wales.

By the early 1870s compliance with the law was high, and the implementation of the new Act in 1875 made no impact at all. In fact, slightly fewer births were registered in 1875 than in 1874. After 1875 a very small number of births still failed to be registered, and even today the General Register Office has procedures to deal with births that have managed to slip through the net.

For the first time, registrars were required to have fixed hours of attendance at a fixed place of business. Previously, the registrar might seek out the new parents at home, or they might call on him at his

*Parish clerk.* (Douglas Jerrold (ed.), *Heads of the People: Portraits of the English,* 1840)

place of business. Many of the first registrars were Poor Law Union officials, especially relieving officers, or doctors, whose work required them to travel around the district. It was therefore not easy to know where they were at any given time.

The registrar would still call on parents at home if they requested it, but there was a 1s fee for this service. When a birth was registered the parents could now obtain for 3d a Certificate of Registry of Birth, showing the name of the child and the date of birth. These are often wrongly referred to as short birth certificates, but true short certificates were not introduced until 1948. Fines for late registration were also revised. Finally, if a child was born to unmarried parents, the father's name could now only appear on the certificate if he accompanied the mother to the register office and signed the register along with her.

The changes to death registration introduced by this Act are often overlooked, but are also significant. A certificate from a doctor was now required to register a death. This measure enabled the collection of more reliable statistics of causes of death; the Statistical Branch was not part of the original General Register Office establishment, but by this time had become a major part of the office's work. Medical certification also discouraged foul play on the part of those with a financial interest in a relative's demise.

There had been a number of well-publicised cases of vulnerable relatives being murdered for an inheritance or for insurance money. Whether the Act was effective in dealing with this problem or not is debatable, since these cases did not suddenly come to a halt in 1875. The new rule did mean that there had to be an actual death to register. Burial registers might not record very much information, but they did at least require the presence of a body to be buried. All that was required to register a death between 1837 and 1874 was that a death was reported to the registrar. Fraudsters spotted this significant loophole as early as 1838, when the first cases came to light of entirely fictitious deaths being registered in order to obtain a death certificate that could be presented to a burial club or insurance company. The 'deceased' in these cases might still be living, or might never have existed at all.

At the local level, financial provision was finally made for registrars to index their own register books. This had been overlooked in the original legislation, and was set at the rate of 7s per book.

It had taken nearly four decades, but most of the flaws in the original legislation were now dealt with. The General Register Office still had difficulties keeping up with the level of work that was coming in, and there was still some concern about births being un-recorded, and some other deficiencies in registration. They occasion-ally prosecuted individuals and even registrars for making false or fraudulent entries. These instances were rare, but it was felt that an example should be made occasionally. Somerset House was not an ideal headquarters for the General Register Office; it was too hot in summer, too cold in winter, and suffered at least one rat infestation. On the whole, though, the system that was set up by the first Registrar General, Thomas Henry Lister, and refined by his successor, George Graham, was working fairly well. Graham was the longest-serving Registrar General, and retired in 1880, shortly after the retire-ment of William Farr, his deputy and Superintendent of Statistics. The pair had worked closely together for nearly forty years, and made a formidable partnership. Graham was succeeded by Brydges Henniker, whose tenure was not regarded as a great success. Graham was a hard act to follow.

---

## Thomas Henry Lister

Thomas Henry Lister came from a very well-connected family; he was the son of Thomas Lister of Armitage Park in Staffordshire, whose cousin, also called Thomas Lister, was the first Baron Ribbles-dale. Thomas Henry's half-sister Adelaide married the second Baron Ribblesdale, yet another Thomas, and after his death she married Lord John Russell, who was Home Secretary at the time. A year later in 1836 it was he who appointed Lister, now his brother-in-law, to the post of Registrar General.

At the time Lister was better known as a romantic novelist, and his works included *Granby* (1826), *Arlington* (1832) and *Anne Grey* (1834). He was educated at Westminster School, and at Trinity College, Cambridge, and on 6 November 1830 he married Lady Mary Theresa

Villiers, a descendant of the statesman Edward Hyde, First Earl of Clarendon. Clarendon was a supporter of the Royalist cause in the Civil War who later became the father-in-law of James II. In 1837 Lister published the three-volume *Life and Administration of Edward, First Earl of Clarendon: with original correspondence and authentic papers never before published*.

While his family connections were undoubtedly of great assistance to him, Lister was a man of proven ability, and had served as a member of the Commission into Education in Ireland which resulted in the establishment of the Model School system there. On being appointed Registrar General, he was faced with the task of setting up an entirely new system and a department to run it. He understood the importance of creating a system that would return accurate and consistent results from the whole country, and he set out his vision in his first Report of the Registrar General in 1838:

> In order to insure in these operations as much uniformity as varying local circumstances would admit, and to facilitate such communication on the subject of divisions as must necessarily precede my ultimate approval, I addressed a Circular Letter to all such Boards of Guardians, pointing out the general principles by which, in the formation of districts, it was advisable to be guided, and the nature of the information with which, in examining the proposed divisions, I must require to be furnished.

He went on to describe in some detail the reasoning behind the administrative framework he had set up for the business of registration. He applied the same attention to detail in his meticulous planning for the 1841 census, a task that he took on at rather short notice, when John Rickman, who had organised the censuses of 1801 to 1831, died suddenly in 1840.

The foundations that he set for both civil registration and census taking were sound, and on the whole stood the test of time. Inevitably, there were problems with the practice that were not covered by the theory, but these were remarkably few, considering the scale of the tasks concerned. Sadly, he did not live to see his creations develop to maturity since he died of tuberculosis on 5 June 1842, aged only 42. He is buried in Kensal Green Cemetery.

Dictionary of National Biography
www.oxforddnb.com/view/article/16768

## George Graham

George Graham, the second Registrar General, held that post for nearly four decades, much longer than any of his successors. He was appointed in 1842 following the death of his predecessor, Thomas Henry Lister. If Lister had laid the foundations for civil registration, it was Graham who completed the structure. He was ably assisted by his Superintendent of Statistics, Dr William Farr, who later also became his deputy. In some ways Graham's reputation was overshadowed by that of Farr, but in reality the two men worked very effectively as a team, and most of their achievements are joint efforts.

The introduction to *Vital Statistics*, a collection of Farr's writings published in 1885, describes Graham:

> Major Graham possessed in an exceptional degree the power of organization, with strong business capacity, and gave close and laborious attention to detail; these combined qualifications made him eminently fitted to be the administrative chief of nearly 3000 registration officers, and of a central office with a staff of nearly 100 clerks of different grades. He felt the deepest interest in the success of civil registration over which he so ably presided, and scarcely less interest in the welfare of those who served under him. The services of Major Graham, in the eyes of the public, who are singularly ignorant about the inner working of government departments, were to some extent overshadowed by the well-deserved esteem in which Dr Farr's talents and services, in utilising the results of civil registration, were held by the public and the press.

George Graham was born in 1801 in Netherby, Cumberland. Like his predecessor he was closely related to the Home Secretary who appointed him, in this case it was his brother, Sir James Graham. But like Lister, he was highly competent at his job. His previous experience in the East India Company's army stood him in good stead as a manager of a large department. He was a shrewd judge of character, and had a good eye for detail. One of his first acts as Registrar General was to notice that there was no system for checking the amount the office spent on postage, and that Mr Rose, the Office Keeper, had taken advantage of this weakness and embezzled large sums of money.

*George Graham, the Second Registrar General, portrait in oils by Frank Holl, 1880.*
(Government Art Collection)

To Graham's annoyance, the ever-cautious Treasury Solicitor did not believe there was enough evidence to prosecute him, but he was allowed to resign. Graham was quick to spot the failings of his staff, but was often prepared to give them a second chance, and went to some effort to obtain *ex gratia* payments from the Treasury for staff who were not entitled to pensions, but whom he considered to be deserving cases.

Graham retired at the end of 1879, and his last act as Registrar General was to ask that Dr Farr, whose health was failing, be retired on full pay, in recognition of his services. Graham died at his home in Belgrave Square in London on 20 May 1888.

Dictionary of National Biography
www.oxforddnb.com/view/article/75323

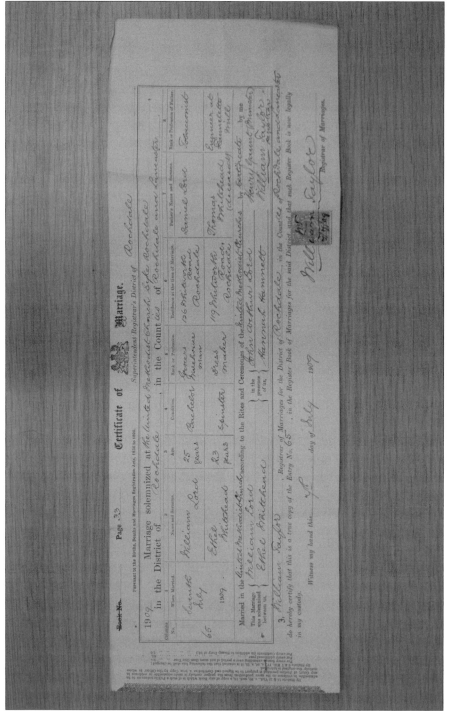

*William Lord and Ethel Whitehead were married in a Methodist church in Rochdale in 1909. This copy was used as evidence in their subsequent divorce case in 1919. (The National Archives J77/1552/8094)*

## William Farr

William Farr rose from humble origins to become a well-respected figure in Victorian England. He was born in Shropshire in 1807, the son of a farm labourer. The local squire, Joseph Pryce, spotted the boy's potential and paid for his education, first at school and then his training as a doctor in Shrewsbury and Paris. He qualified as a physician in 1832, and married in the following year. He set up a medical practice in London and supplemented his income by writing articles in the *Lancet* and other journals.

In 1838 he took up a post in the new General Register Office as an abstractor of statistics. This was initially a temporary appointment, but in 1839 he was made a permanent member of the establishment, and rose to become Superintendent of Statistics and eventually Deputy Registrar General. He was responsible for the way that the statistics were reported, and often added commentaries to the annual Report of the Registrar General on statistical trends and developed many of the standard methods of modern vital statistics and epidemiology.

His activities were not confined to his work at the General Register Office, and he was a prominent member of the Statistical Society of London, which later became the Royal Statistical Society, and was its president in 1871 and 1872. He also worked closely with Florence Nightingale on hospital and Army sanitary reform. His greatest partnership was with Registrar General George Graham, with whom he worked for thirty-seven years at the General Register Office. Their skills complemented each other, and between them they shaped the way that the office worked for many years to come. When George Graham retired at the end of 1879 he wrote, 'in this my last Official communication to their Lordships I venture to express an earnest wish that his excellent services may be recognized with special consideration, and that he may be permitted to receive Full Pay during the rest of his life', and a later commentator said, 'it is pleasant to refer to the "entente cordiale" which marked the long continued official relations between these two eminent civil servants'.

Graham was concerned for the welfare of his friend and colleague, who was not wealthy and still had unmarried daughters to support. Farr applied for the vacant post of Registrar General, and the medical establishment was outraged when he was passed over for the underqualified Brydges Henniker. But for all Farr's talents as a medical statistician, he did not have the management and organisational skill required for such a job, and he was now in his 70s and his health was failing. In 1881 he too retired, and was made Companion of the Bath and received the British Medical Association's gold medal.

A Testimonial Fund was set up for him, the contributors including George Graham, Brydges Henniker, Florence Nightingale and Charles Darwin. He died on 14 April 1883 at his home in Maida Vale, and is buried in the churchyard of Bromley Common, along with his second wife. A volume of his collected writings, *Vital Statistics*, was published in 1885.

Dictionary of National Biography
www.oxforddnb.com/view/article/9185

Henniker held the post for twenty years, during which time the workload of the office continued to grow. Legislation was proposed to allow Nonconformist clergy to perform marriages, but the first attempt in 1893 was so badly worded that it was abandoned. The law was finally changed in 1898 by the Authorised Persons Act, which allowed individuals to become registered to perform marriages, so that a registrar need not be present at marriages in Nonconformist places of worship. Arrangements were made to compensate the registrars for their resulting loss of income, since they were now only required to perform register office marriages and attend where the place of worship had no Authorised Person of its own. This change in the law also brought some problems; like the Anglican clergy in 1837, the newly appointed Authorised Persons had little experience or training in their registration duties, and the quality of the quarterly returns left something to be desired: 'The certified Copies of Marriages solemnized since April last by about one thousand Authorised Persons are now being received in this office, and they naturally display an infinite variety of blunders and contraventions of the Rules and Regulations of a more or less serious character.'

Later on it emerged that there was some misunderstanding of the new law. Church of England clergy were automatically empowered to perform marriages as soon as they were ordained, and many Nonconformist clergy believed that the same rules now applied to them. But this was not the case, since the new Act required that each individual applied to be registered as an Authorised Person. As a result, some newly appointed Nonconformist clergy unwittingly celebrated a number of marriages before they were legally entitled to do so. The marriages concerned were validated by periodic pieces of retrospective legislation, and the parties were almost certainly blissfully unaware of their temporary 'unmarried' status.

The extra pressure on the General Register Office was not just in the quantity of births, marriages and deaths to be registered, but in the volume of searches in the indexes and applications for certificates. Henniker did not have as firm a grasp on the work of the office as his predecessor, and as a result the search room staff had become lax in their application of the rules. The wording of the original Act was quite clear in allowing that information could only be given in the form of certified copies. In practice, however, it had become the custom for clerks to allow applicants to view the entries before purchasing certificates.

This was greatly to the advantage of the applicants, since the index information was often insufficient to identify the right entry and it could take several attempts before the right one was obtained. Many of these applicants were clerks from law firms and insurance companies, and the companies undoubtedly put pressure on the search-room staff to allow these unauthorised verifications which saved their firms considerable sums of money. This finally came to light when it was realised that the revenue from certificate production was far below the level that would be expected from the greatly increased rate of searches in the indexes. As a result, the rules were properly enforced again from 1898, much to the annoyance of many searchers. Questions were even asked in Parliament about the Registrar General's arbitrary action in changing the rules, but, unfortunately for researchers then and now, he was only enforcing a rule that had always existed, and is still in place today.

The first significant measure of the twentieth century was not to do with registration law as such: the long-overdue Deceased Wife's Sister Marriage Act was passed in 1907, which finally allowed a widower to marry the sister of his dead wife. Previously there had

## Brydges Powell Henniker

The third Registrar General, like his two predecessors, came from a wealthy and aristocratic family. The now dormant Henniker baronetcy of Newton Hall in Essex was created in 1813 for his grandfather, Brydges Trescothick Henniker, who had represented Kildare in the Irish Parliament that was dissolved in 1801.

Brydges Henniker was born in 1835, the son of the third baronet, Augustus Brydges Henniker, and he inherited the baronetcy from him in 1849. He held the post of Registrar General for twenty years, and only his immediate predecessor George Graham and Sylvanus Vivian (1921–45) served for longer. He was educated at Eton, and like Graham had served in the Army, in the 68th Regiment of Foot, the Horse Guards and as a captain in the West Essex Yeomanry.

Like Lister, he had also worked in government service as private secretary to the President of the Local Government Board. The board had been formed in 1871 by combining the Poor Law Board, the Local Government Act Office and the Medical Department of the Privy Council. At the same time, the new body also assumed control of the General Register Office, previously the responsibility of the Home Office.

Henniker is not generally regarded as a very effective Registrar General, lacking the skills of George Graham in making the office's case to the Treasury, and simultaneously managing an increasingly troublesome workforce. Graham was a very hard act to follow, and Henniker also had to work without the assistance of William Farr, who had been such a support to Graham. Even a more talented man than Henniker would have had difficulty in steering the General Register Office through the closing decades of the nineteenth century. The medical and statistical authorities were hostile to him from the start, for taking a job that they believed should have gone to Farr, their favoured candidate, or at least to someone with medical or statistical expertise. Henniker had neither, and as it turned out was not a very good manager either.

The annual Reports of the Registrar General were noticeably shorter and drier in content than those published in Graham's time, and expressed no opinions or vision for improving public health in the future, which had been so characteristic of Graham's forcefully expressed views. He was less successful than Graham in obtaining

Treasury funding for the General Register Office's increasing work-load, and the hard-pressed staff, discontented with his weak manage-ment, complained directly to the Treasury about their poor pay and prospects.

At best he pursued a 'more of the same' policy, and there were no significant innovations or improvements during his time. He did redeem himself to a degree when he, uncharacteristically, did not defer to the Local Government Board when they wanted to destroy the manuscript returns for the 1851 and 1861 census. He commented that if the records were from 1751 or 1761 they would be regarded as highly valuable, showing that he had a sense of historical perspective, even if he lacked the advocacy or management skills to make effective use of it in the interests of his department.

been a number of illegal marriages of this kind, many of which remained undetected, but if drawn to the attention of the authorities would result in prosecution. Other couples in this situation, knowing they could not marry legally, chose instead to live together, often claiming to be man and wife. The corresponding legislation allowing a widow to marry her deceased husband's brother was not passed until 1921.

Important changes in a number of areas were made by the Births and Deaths Registration Act of 1926. These included for the first time the registration of stillborn children. This register and its indexes are not open to public inspection, and the only people who can obtain information from it are the parents of a stillborn infant, or the infant's siblings if the parents are no longer alive. The Legitimacy Act of the same year allowed for the re-registration of a birth following the marriage of the parents of child born out of wedlock, thereby making the child legitimate. This option was not open to every couple, since the re-registration could only take place if the parents had been free to marry at the time of the child's birth. Where a birth is re-registered, the original index entry should be annotated with a reference to the new entry, and the same certificate will be produced regardless of which index entry is quoted in the application. There can sometimes be many years between the original birth and the re-registration.

Late registration of births had been allowed in both the 1836 and 1874 Acts, initially requiring the Registrar General's authority after six months, extended to twelve months by the 1874 Act. Neither specified an upper time limit, whereas legislation covering births overseas and at sea had a limit of seven years. In practice, the Registrar General did not at first grant permission any later than seven years, but this was relaxed during the twentieth century, as it became much harder for a person to operate in the modern world without this vital documentation. Very late registration was still at the discretion of the Registrar General, and an extremely high standard of proof was required to make such a registration, but there are isolated instances of births being registered more than fifty years late.

As the twentieth century progressed, the General Register Office faced a number of challenges. The introduction of old-age pensions in 1908 increased the number of applications for birth and marriage certificates needed as proof of age. There was also the practical matter of carrying out the business of registration during the two world wars. In common with many other employers, the office lost a number of male staff to the armed forces, and some of them were replaced by women. The General Register Office had employed a number of female staff since the turn of the century, but now their numbers and the range of jobs that they did increased. The wars also placed extra burdens on the registration service in the form of the increased death registrations, and also of increased applications for marriage certificates by war widows who needed them for pension purposes.

With the Second World War came a new set of issues brought about by the bombing of the civilian population. Not only were there many more deaths than usual to register, but the register offices and Somerset House itself were at risk from bombing raids. The General Register Office was evacuated from London to the safety of Smedley Hydro in Southport, which is still the home of certificate production. At one time there was even a suggestion that a public search room should be set up there, but this never happened, and the building has only ever been open to the public on occasional open days. Some register offices were damaged by bombing, but fortunately very few actual registers were destroyed, and in the great majority of cases the ordinary registration system ensured that there were duplicate copies elsewhere. With the evacuation of children and their mothers from cities to the countryside, a number of births took place that could not be registered in the district where they had occurred, and special instructions were issued to registrars to cope with these.

During the war there was a suggestion that marriage by proxy might be introduced, a practice that was allowed in some countries. The motivation for this was to legitimise children whose parents were not married and whose fathers were serving abroad. If the man died overseas then the child could never be legitimised by the marriage of the parents as the law stood, and a proxy marriage might be a solution to this. This was given serious consideration but was eventually rejected on the grounds of the legal complications that might ensue. For example, if one of the parties changed their mind or died between agreeing to the marriage and the ceremony taking place, the legal status of the marriage would be uncertain.

Another issue that arose during wartime was the rise in the number of applications for corrections to be made to entries in the birth registers. There has always been provision for corrections to be made where there is an error of fact or substance in the original entry and, in wartime, circumstances arose where this was more prevalent than before. When a birth is registered by a married woman, her husband is deemed to be the father unless there is an explicit statement to the contrary. During the war, a number of men returned home to find they were shown as the father of a child conceived and born while they were overseas. The Registrar General's correspondence contains samples of requests by these men to have their names removed from the birth entries.

After the Second World War there was a complete overhaul of registration districts, after a century and more of piecemeal altera-tions. Since registrars had become salaried in the 1920s this could now be done without complicated compensation provision for those who lost income as a result.

Somerset House was no longer big enough to accommodate the increasing number of registers and indexes, and in 1974 the General Register Office moved its public search room to nearby St Catherine's House, but this too became overcrowded, and in the late 1980s certificate production was moved from there to the Southport office.

Now the search room was full of family historians, and was becoming increasingly congested. Interest in the subject continued to rise, and in 1997 the search room was moved to the new Family Records Centre in Islington, sharing the premises with the Central London search rooms of the Public Record Office, which at the same time vacated its premises in Chancery Lane. There they remained until the Family Records Centre itself closed in 2008, and there is no longer a General Register Office public search room. Most people now access the indexes up to 2005 online – the more recent ones can only be viewed on microfiche.

*Chapter 6*

# CIVIL REGISTRATION, PART 3:
## 'Indexes of the Registers to be Made and Kept in the General Register Office'

W e find references to the birth, marriage and death certificates that we need by searching for them in the indexes produced by the General Register Office, or by the local registration services. The references from the index are then used to produce a certified copy of the entry concerned. This is the way that searchers have used the General Register Office records since they began in 1837, but in recent years there have been some subtle but significant changes to this process. First of all, when we search the indexes we may be looking at microfiche or microfilm versions of the original index books, but we are more likely to be doing our searching online. This means that we are instead interrogating a database, which is not the same thing. The existence of online indexes means that searches now take a fraction of the time that they used to, but there is still merit in searching the indexes in the old-fashioned way. An under-standing of the way they were constructed can help you make the most of your online searching.

Understanding the indexes may also help to explain why an entry cannot be found, or to identify the most likely one where there are several possible candidates. Sometimes it is worth checking scans or films of the index pages where you suspect there may have been transcription errors or even omissions in the online versions. Between the details of a birth, death or marriage being written in an original register and the version that appears in an online database, the information could have been copied as many as six times. Every time that a copy is made, whether by transcription or by physical means such as carbon copies or photocopying, some errors are bound to creep in. Even if the proportion of errors is tiny, in the context of the millions of entries in General Register Office registers this still represents a very considerable number.

The General Register Office indexes of births, marriages and deaths have often been criticised for their incompleteness and inaccuracy, and up to a point this is justified. Mike Foster illustrated this in some detail in his 1998 book *A Comedy of Errors, or, The Marriage Records of England and Wales, 1837–1899*, and in a second volume published in 2003. The fault does not lie entirely with the General Register Office, however, and the system of indexing that was set up by Thomas Henry Lister, and refined by his successors, was rather a good one. Unfortunately, the office was always short of the resources needed to put it into operation. When registration began, no one really knew how many events would be registered under this completely new system; in fact this was rather the point of setting it up, the problem being that the existing methods were inadequate as a measure of the numbers of births, marriages and deaths taking place each year in England and Wales.

As early as 1838, when the first indexes were being prepared, Lister was pleading with the Treasury for extra funds to employ more staff, or at least to be able to pay overtime to his existing staff. Notwithstanding the opposition to civil registration from some quarters, the volume of work coming in to the office was more than it could cope with, and a backlog was already building up. This was a constant theme for many decades to come, with frequent appeals from successive Registrars General for more resources. Sometimes these would be successful, but this was a department that, for at least the remainder of the nineteenth century, was constantly struggling to catch up with the increasing volume of work coming its way.

The method of collating and indexing births, marriages and deaths that was established in Lister's day remained largely unchanged until 1969, when computers were first used for index preparation. There were changes in the presentation of the indexes, still visible today in the images of the finished pages, but the underlying principles were remarkably constant. At the end of every quarter, registrars, Church of England clergy, Secretaries of Synagogues and Quaker Registering Officers were required to make copies of every event they had registered during that period, or a nil return if there were no entries. These were sent to Somerset House where an army of clerks would abstract the names and prepare the index pages that were bound into volumes and placed on the search-room shelves.

The 'quarterly returns', as they were known, were loose sheets of paper with the same layout as the register books, with ten entries per page of births and deaths. Marriage registers were a little different; the original registers have always had two entries to a page, but for the first few years of registration the loose sheets used for the quarterly returns had four entries. This was reduced to two in 1853 to save on storage space. When the returns arrived at Somerset House they were checked to see that the numbered entries followed on from those of the previous quarter from that district. Next, they were checked for obvious errors, such as a registration date earlier than a birth date, but the clerks were not mind-readers, so they could not check for incorrect information caused by copying errors.

The returns were then arranged within each registration district, alphabetically by sub-district for births and deaths, and by place for marriages. The places of marriage were Church of England parishes first, then the registrars' marriages and any Jewish or Quaker marriages. From 1899 some Nonconformist places of worship also had their own marriage registers. Returns for registration districts were then arranged in regional groupings and the pages were numbered. The volumes were also numbered, and these are the volume and page numbers that appear in the indexes. The volume numbers were Roman numerals I to XXIV until 1853 when a combination of Arabic numerals and letters was used from 1a to 11b. In both cases the numbering started with the London area, working outwards from there and ending with Wales. Since 1945 there have been a number of revisions of registration districts and reference systems.

Reminders were sent to registrars and clergy who had not sent in their returns, but the indexing could not be held up indefinitely, so some very late returns arrived after the indexing had been done and the pages had to be inserted in the appropriate place; these are the

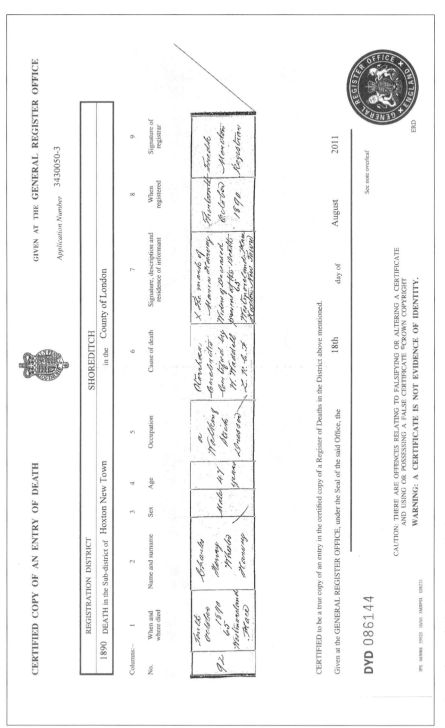

*Death certificate of Charles Henry Wheeler Harvey, 1890.* (General Register Office Q4 1890, Shoreditch 1c 53)

page numbers that end in a, b, c and so on. If they arrived even later, once the indexes had been compiled, the entries from these pages would also have to be hand-written into the completed volumes, or 'interlined'.

Once the volumes were prepared, the indexing could begin, starting with the work of the transcribers. They copied the surname, forenames, registration district, volume and page numbers for each entry onto special transcription forms, and the completed forms were then cut into slips. Now it was the turn of the sorters, who arranged the slips into alphabetical order. This was monotonous work, and it must have been hard for the sorters to maintain concentration, often for six days a week. The sorted slips were then passed to the indexers, who copied the names and references onto parchment pages which were bound into volumes and placed on the shelves of the public search room at Somerset House. There was no change in the way the indexes were compiled until 1866, when the indexes were printed for the first time. It is a tribute to the durability of the parchment pages that most of them were still in daily use until 2007, when the volumes were withdrawn from use and placed in storage.

In 1866 the transcribing and sorting stages remained the same as before, but with the age at death being added to the death indexes. Forenames, which had been recorded in full, were now limited to one, with initials only for the rest, although in 1867 the second forename was restored. The work previously done in-house by the indexers was now outsourced to Darling & Co., printers, in the East End of London, who typeset the new printed indexes directly from the bundles of sorted slips. For the first time it was possible to produce more than one copy of the indexes.

The work of the clerks involved in index preparation was checked at every stage, at least in theory. In reality, however, this was not always done; there certainly was some checking, as evidenced by pencil marks that are visible on the original parchment pages, though sadly not on film, fiche or scanned copies of them. Each batch of eight parchment pages bore the name of the indexer who compiled them, and sometimes the name or initials of the senior clerk who checked his work, with the number of errors found.

The paucity of information in the indexes had been partly addressed by the addition of the age at death to the death indexes in 1866, but the next improvement was not until 1911, when the mother's maiden name was added to the birth indexes and the spouse's surname to the marriage indexes. Unfortunately, the number of fore-names was again reduced to one, with initials for the rest. No further changes were made until 1969 when computers were first used to prepare the indexes, and the second forename was restored. Death

**"THEN THE FACE OF THE CLERK WILL BE COVERED WITH A SMILE."**

*GRO Clerk 2, 1899.*
(*New Penny Magazine*, 1899)

indexes now gave the full date of birth, and both birth and death certificates were redesigned to provide more information. The new death certificates are particularly helpful to the genealogist, since they also give the place of birth, and the maiden name of a widow or married woman.

In 1984 the first 'born digital' indexes were produced, and indexes from that date are in database format. They were also produced as printed annual volumes, not quarterly as before, and the referencing system was changed to reflect this, showing the month of registration as part of the reference. Online indexes 1984 to 2005 are available on several commercial websites, and birth and death indexes for 2006 are online at www.findmypast.co.uk.

The General Register Office no longer supplies online index data to commercial companies, so there are no more recent indexes online. There is no longer a General Register Office search room and there is no public access to the printed indexes, but microfiche versions of the most recent indexes are supplied to seven designated repositories throughout England and Wales, namely:

- Birmingham Central Library
- Bridgend Reference and Information Library
- The British Library
- City of Westminster Archives Centre
- London Metropolitan Archives
- Greater Manchester County Record Office
- Plymouth Central Library

When you order a certificate online from the General Register Office, it is important that you select the correct date range, otherwise the reference for your certificate will not fit the boxes provided.

From 1837 to 1983 a reference comprises four elements – year, quarter, volume and page. It is not a reference to a specific entry, but to a page in the register book compiled from the quarterly returns at the General Register Office. Birth and death registers have ten entries to a page, and marriage registers four to a page until 1852 and two from then on. So if two birth entries with the same surname also have exactly the same reference, this may sometimes, but not always, indicate twins. Two children with the same surname might be on the same page but could have been registered days or even weeks apart. Conversely, the first twin could be at the bottom of a page, and their twin at the top of the next.

When searching for a marriage the entries for the bride and groom must have identical references, indicating that they are on the same page, but this is not an absolute guarantee that they married each other. Occasionally, an application for a marriage certificate will be rejected as 'unrelated' where the names are from two different marriages that just happen to be on the same page. This is obviously more likely in the early years with four marriages to a page, and with very common names.

Although they withstood constant handling on a daily basis, in a succession of public search rooms, the General Register Office was concerned about the wear and tear on the indexes. Some volumes were re-typed in the 1960s and the parchment versions withdrawn.

The General Register Office's indexes have been microfilmed by the Genealogical Society of Utah and the films have been made available through Family History Centers worldwide. They should not be confused with the micro*fiche* set of indexes produced by the General Register Office in the 1980s.

## Chapter 7

# NONCONFORMIST REGISTERS:
## 'That All Registers and Records Deposited in the General Register Office by Virtue of this Act Shall be Receivable in Evidence in all Courts of Justice'

The history of Nonconformity in England and Wales is long and complex, stretching back as far as the English Reformation and the establishment of the Church of England under Henry VIII. Strictly speaking, a Nonconformist can be defined as anyone whose religious beliefs do not conform to those of the official state Church, but in the family history world, the term is usually understood to refer to members of one of the many dissenting Protestant communities that emerged in the mid-to-late seventeenth century.

The Restoration of the monarchy in 1660 signalled the end of Puritanism as a discrete religious movement in England and Wales. However, the underlying concerns held by certain sections of the population regarding the way in which the established Church of England was run continued to grow and the people who held these concerns came to be known as Nonconformists.

This growth came about despite continuing attempts to repress all forms of religious dissent – attempts that intensified with the passing of the Test and Corporation Acts in 1673 and 1661 respectively. Between them, these closely associated Acts effectively debarred Nonconformists from taking up positions of political influence, both locally and nationally, by stipulating that only those who were willing to 'receive the sacrament of the Lord's Supper according to the rites of the Church of England' were eligible to sit on public bodies.

But the State was always fighting a losing battle and in 1689 the Act of Toleration was passed which gave basic freedom of worship to Protestant Nonconformists. One of the results of this more tolerant attitude was that many of these Protestant congregations began to keep records of the births or baptisms and deaths or burials of members of their own religious communities.

A small number of Nonconformist registers survive from the period of the English Civil War but these are the exceptions rather than the rule. Many of the surviving registers don't start until the late eighteenth century and some run for just a few years up to 1837.

The earliest registers are often little more than notebooks but since many of the ministers of the new congregations were Puritan clergymen who had been ejected from their parishes at the Restoration, they tended to adhere to the formats used by the Church of England.

The standard of record keeping in the surviving Nonconformist registers is generally good but the amount of detail recorded varies greatly. As a rule, you would expect to find as much information as in the equivalent Church of England registers and in many cases much more. It is not uncommon for dates of birth as well as baptism to be recorded and mothers' maiden names frequently appear.

By the early 1800s Nonconformists made up almost a quarter of the population of England and Wales and there was a growing sense of injustice about the unequal treatment afforded them.

In the early years of the nineteenth century, the campaign for the repeal of the hated Test and Corporation Acts started to gather pace. As well as restricting their opportunities in public life, the Acts prevented Dissenters from attending universities and from becoming Members of Parliament or commissioned officers in the Royal Navy or the British Army. And for many Nonconformists the fact that their registers continued to have no legal status was a constant source of annoyance.

The Napoleonic Wars proved a turning point. It was generally accepted that the thousands of Nonconformists who had served as soldiers and sailors in the British armed forces fully deserved the same rights and opportunities as the men they had fought alongside

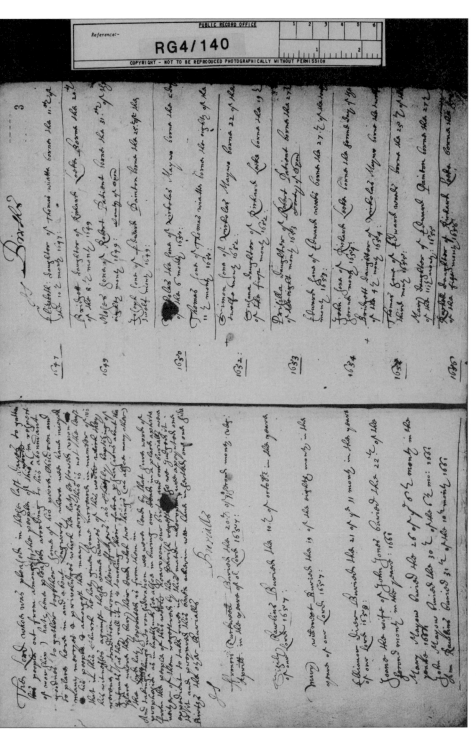

*Register of the Baptist chapel at Coate, Oxfordshire with entries beginning in 1647. (The National Archives RG4/140 folio 3)*

who attended Church of England services. And this, combined with the increasing influence of Nonconformists in fields such as the arts, science and commerce, lent considerable weight to the movement.

But the beginnings of the campaign can be traced back to events that took place nearly a hundred years before the Battle of Waterloo. Dr Daniel Williams, a Presbyterian minister, was one of the most prominent and influential Nonconformists of his time and when he died in 1716 a trust was established under the terms of his will which, among other things, enabled a library to be set up dedicated to the study of Protestant Nonconformity. The library, which bears his name, is still in existence today and is a prime resource for anyone researching the history of Protestant Nonconformity in England and Wales.

Dr Williams had also been involved in establishing a pressure group known as the General Body of the Three Denominations which aimed to represent the collective interests of the Presbyterians, Independents and Baptists. After his death, the group's influence continued to grow, lobbying Parliament and gaining friends in high places.

One of the most significant acts of the General Body was the establishment of a Dissenters' birth registry. In 1742 it was announced that a registry had been opened, at Dr Williams' Library, which would allow Protestant Dissenters the opportunity of registering the births of their children and to have certified copies (i.e. certificates) of the entries. The amount of detail recorded was remarkable for the time. In addition to the name of the child, the date and place of his or her birth and the parents' names, most of the records also show the mother's maiden name and, in many cases, *her* parents' names as well. The father's occupation and the precise place of the child's birth are also usually given.

The registry (formally known as the General Register of Protestant Dissenters) maintained two sets of records. There were two copies of the birth certificate produced, one of which was given to the family and the other retained at Dr Williams' Library. The details were then copied into a register which was also kept at the Library. In essence, this was a prototype for the system that was ultimately adopted by the General Register Office when civil registration was introduced in 1837.

Over the 95 years that the registry was in existence, almost 50,000 births were recorded. Retrospective registration was encouraged and although the registry was opened in 1742, an entry for a birth occurring as early as 1716 appears in the records and several registrations of people aged 50 or more have been found.

It had been hoped that the records created by the registry would in time be recognised by the State as legal records of birth. However, this didn't happen until after the introduction of civil registration in 1837 when the registry was closed and its records were authenticated by the first Non-parochial Registers Commission.

The Test and Corporation Acts were eventually repealed in 1828 and full equality (as far as registration of life events was concerned) was achieved in July 1837 when the Act for registering Births, Deaths, and Marriages in England was passed and civil registration was introduced. For the first time since 1753, Nonconformists would be able to perform their own marriage ceremonies, and births and deaths would now be registered regardless of religious persuasion.

And it was one of the first tasks of the newly established General Register Office to set up a commission (known as the Non-parochial Registers Commission) to look into the state and extent of the Nonconformists' registers and, more significantly, to ask the various congregations to submit their registers to the General Register Office for authentication.

A contemporary piece in the *Gentleman's Magazine* of October 1840 discussed the work of the Commission,

> 7000 registers, principally those of congregations of Protestant Dissenters, were reported upon as sufficiently authentic to be preserved and admitted as evidence in all courts of justice; and by this Bill it is provided that these registers shall be deposited in the custody of the Registrar General, and that the originals or certified extracts from them may be used in courts of law and sessions, and in courts of equity.

This vast collection of registers eventually found its way into the Public Record Office (now The National Archives), along with the other records created or inherited by the General Register Office.

There are very few marriages recorded in these registers after 1753. Hardwicke's Marriage Act required that marriages were to take place in a parish church, so Nonconformists (with the exception of Quakers) were forced to marry within the Church of England in order to ensure that their marriages were legally valid and that their children were legitimate.

Not all Nonconformist congregations were willing to surrender their registers to the 1837 Commission and in 1857 a further attempt was made to gather in those registers that had been missed earlier. The second Non-parochial Registers Commission collected another 300 or so registers.

## Quakers

Among the earliest of the groups that we now recognise as Protestant Nonconformists was the Society of Friends – better known to us as the Quakers. The precise date of the establishment of the Quaker movement is impossible to pinpoint but what is certain is that one man, George Fox, was more responsible than any other for the founding of the Society of Friends. Fox was born in 1624, and as a young man he was one of many itinerant preachers who travelled around the British Isles in the middle years of the seventeenth century, seeking religious meaning and openly questioning the doctrines of the Established Church.

Perhaps unsurprisingly, George Fox and others like him were not exactly welcomed with open arms by the English Church and State. In 1649 he was imprisoned for the first time but gradually, throughout the 1650s, the movement that ultimately evolved into the Society of Friends started to take shape as more and more people began to follow Fox and his teachings. In 1652 he preached to a meeting of over a thousand in Westmoreland and despite a succession of imprisonments for blasphemy, Fox started to gain more influential friends including Oliver Cromwell himself. The first formal structured Quaker meetings were held at around this time.

In 1662 the Quaker Act was passed which effectively outlawed the Quaker movement by making it illegal to refuse to take the Oath of

Allegiance to the king and State; an oath that Quakers were quite simply unable to take.

The persecutions continued and during the reign of Charles II more than 13,000 Quakers were arrested and imprisoned, a situation that led to large numbers of Friends emigrating to America. However, the outlook for the Quakers gradually improved and when Hardwicke's Marriage Act was passed in 1753, uniquely among Protestant Nonconformists, the Quakers were explicitly exempted and were therefore free to marry within their own meeting houses.

The first Non-parochial Registers Commission collected no fewer than 1,445 registers from the Society of Friends. The Quakers had devised a sophisticated system of registering births, marriages and deaths which was based on their own hierarchical structure of Quarterly (regional) and Monthly (local) meetings. In theory, therefore, each event should be recorded twice. The amount of detail recorded in Quaker registers can be extensive; later marriages, for example, often include the names of both sets of parents as well as the occupations and residences of the witnesses.

An interesting feature of the Quakers' records is that the certificates are often 'witnessed' by scores of relatives and other members of the local meeting, providing a unique insight into the social networks of the Society of Friends.

## Presbyterians, Congregationalists and Baptists

The Presbyterians, Baptists and Congregationalists can all trace their origins to the European Reformation of the mid-to-late sixteenth century, but it wasn't until after the Restoration that they began to attract large numbers of ordinary people who were, for one reason or another, disaffected with the Church of England.

Presbyterianism, a doctrine that was heavily influenced by the teachings of John Calvin and John Knox, was first established in England as early as 1572 and although the earliest Presbyterian groups met in secret, the movement gradually moved into the open. In 1647, during the Long Parliament, an Act was passed that legalised Presbyterianism but the return of the monarchy saw the movement return to the status of Nonconformity. The earliest Nonconformist register held by The National Archives is that of the Presbyterian Chapel at Hindley near Wigan in Lancashire which commences in 1642.

The Congregationalists (also known as Independents) can trace their origins to the early 1580s when the theologian Robert Browne attempted to start a church in Norwich. Browne was arrested and forced to flee the country for the Netherlands but he remained influential and a number of his followers took up his work. In 1639, as Congregationalism became more widespread, the first Independent Church in Wales was opened and five years later, the oldest surviving Independent register (that of the Bull Lane Independent Chapel in Stepney, East London) begins with the baptism of 'John the son of Captain John Robinson of Shorditch', who was baptised on the '15th Day of the 10th month 1644'.

The story of the origins of the English Baptist Church is highly complex. John Smyth, an English pastor based in Amsterdam in the early 1600s, is generally considered to be the founder of the movement. The villages of Coate and Longworth on the Oxfordshire/ Berkshire border boast the earliest surviving Baptist register, containing entries dating from 1647. A contemporary note in the register sheds a fascinating light on the thoughts and concerns of these early Nonconformists: 'our births and our burialls were neither of them regestered by the parish regester so we judged it expedient to take care in this mater ...'. Due to the Baptists' belief that adults and not children should be baptised, their registers record births rather than baptisms.

Collectively, the Three Denominations were, as has been seen, at the forefront of the ultimately successful campaign for the repeal of the Test and Corporation Acts.

## Methodists

The eighteenth century saw the birth of another major Nonconformist group. The brothers John and Charles Wesley were brought up by staunch Anglican parents (their father was the rector of Epworth in Lincolnshire) but they shared evangelical beliefs which were often at odds with the strict doctrines of the Established Church. John Wesley became a charismatic and popular preacher whose inspirational open-air sermons attracted huge crowds and he frequently came into conflict with the Church's hierarchy. Despite misgivings held by both brothers, Charles was adamant that they should remain within the Church of England and it wasn't until after John's death in 1791, therefore, that Wesleyan Methodist groups began to emerge.

Registers dating from much earlier than this survive for other Methodist groups such as the Primitive Methodists, New Connexion Methodists and Calvinistic Methodists, but the earliest Wesleyan registers date from the late 1780s and early 1790s.

In 1818, following the example set by the Three Denominations, the Wesleyan Methodists opened their own birth registry, operated along almost identical lines. Over 10,000 births were recorded here in just under 20 years.

## Other Protestant Denominations

Quakers, Presbyterians, Baptists, Congregationalists and the various branches of Methodists may have comprised the major Protestant Nonconformist groups, but there were scores of smaller communities that had a significant part to play in the history of English Non-conformity, the Inghamites, Moravians, Muggletonians, Unitarians and Swedenborgians to name just a few. The National Archives holds registers of several hundred such congregations.

Along with the registers of thousands of individual congregations, the records also include the registers of a number of multi-denominational Nonconformist burial grounds, most notably those of Bunhill Fields in London. Dating back to 1713, the burial registers of Bunhill Fields contain the names of many prominent Non-conformists, including William Blake, Daniel Defoe, John Bunyan and Dr Daniel Williams.

## Roman Catholics

The Act of Toleration of 1689 was not extended to Roman Catholics and it wasn't until the passing of the Catholic Emancipation Act in 1829 that Catholics were granted full freedom of worship.

*Dean Row Nonconformist Chapel.* (J R Green, *A Short History of the English People*, 1894, Vol. 4)

The two Non-parochial Register Commissions also attempted to collect the registers of the various Roman Catholic communities, but, given their long history of persecution, many priests were, perhaps understandably, somewhat reluctant to part with their registers. It's important to note that Roman Catholic registers are used not just as records of past events but as proof, for example, that a person wanting to get married in the Catholic faith was also baptised a Catholic. So there was good reason for the Roman Catholic churches to want to hold on to their registers. As a result, there are fewer than 200 Roman Catholic registers among the records held by The National Archives.

## Non-parochial Registers

The registers collected by the two Commissions are properly referred to as 'non-parochial' registers. The reason for this is that the collection includes a significant number of Church of England registers maintained by organisations that lay outside the usual ecclesiastical parochial structure. Examples of these are the registers of the British Lying-In Hospital; the records of Thomas Coram's Foundling Hospital; the registers of the Chapels Royal at St James's Palace, Whitehall and Windsor Castle and, perhaps most significantly, the registers of the military and naval hospitals at Chelsea and Greenwich.

The National Archives also holds the registers of a number of foreign churches in England and Wales, including an important collection of registers from the Huguenot community. These are among the oldest records in this series with some dating from the late 1500s.

## Other Registers

Many registers that the two Non-parochial Commissions failed to collect, or which were opened after the work of the Commissions was complete, have since been deposited with the relevant county record office or local studies library. The London Metropolitan Archives, for example, holds several hundred registers from the Greater London area. Some churches and chapels still hold their own registers, many of which date back to the nineteenth century or even earlier.

The first Commission also considered the status of an intriguing collection of over 800 registers and notebooks, commonly (but inaccurately) known as the Fleet Marriage Registers. These were the registers and notebooks of a variety of chapels, inns, taverns and 'marriage houses' situated in or around the Fleet Prison in London and a number of other places that were outside the jurisdiction of the Church of England.

More than 250,000 irregular or clandestine marriages are recorded in the registers, dating from the late 1600s up to 1753. Conservative estimates suggest that by the 1740s one in every ten marriages in England was taking place in the Fleet. The country was scandalised

*A Fleet marriage party.* (Charles Knight, *London*, n.d.)

and something had to be done. Hardwicke's Marriage Act finally put an end to clandestine marriages in England and Wales by ordering that all marriages had to take place within the Established Church of England.

In the early 1800s, the surviving Fleet registers were collected and brought together by members of the legal profession, clearly conscious of their potential historical importance. The registers were deposited at the Registry of the Bishop of London in 1821 on the order of the Home Office and were later presented to the General Register Office's First Non-parochial Registers Commission. The Commission decided not to grant the Fleet registers the full authentication awarded to the main collection of Nonconformist registers, but instead they were to be transferred from the Registry into the General Register Office's safe custody. They ultimately ended up in the care of The National Archives.

*Chapter 8*

# OVERSEAS AND AT SEA:
## 'Any Child of an English Parent Born at Sea on Board of a British Vessel'

Some of the trickiest births, marriages and deaths to find are those that took place outside Britain. Many of these relate to members of the armed forces and their families (see Chapter 9), but of course there are lots of other reasons for British people to travel abroad; Britain is a trading nation, and for many years was an imperial one too. Unfortunately, there is no single place where you can hope to find the records of their births, marriages and deaths. Many of them will not be recorded at all in any British source, but only in the country where they occurred. There has never been any legal requirement for events to be registered with British authorities, but for those that were registered, the two biggest collections are those of the General Register Office and of The National Archives. There is some overlap between them.

The Miscellaneous Overseas Collection held by the General Register Office consists of a selection of birth, marriage and death registers of events that took place overseas or at sea, some of them in the form of records kept by the armed services. These records are held and indexed separately from the main series of births, marriages and deaths for England and Wales. However, like the main series, full details of an entry can still only be obtained in the form of a certified copy. It is therefore worth checking other sources first, in case there is a cheaper alternative.

The Miscellaneous Overseas Collection is the only part of the General Register Office that holds records earlier than 1837, in the form of some Army registers starting as early as 1760. These are mainly records of baptisms, marriages and burials kept by Army chaplains, and the entries are similar to those in parish registers of the same period. Some of the Army registers, however, also record events that took place within Britain, which of course included Ireland until 1921. The non-military collection of birth, marriage and death registers held by the General Register Office is as follows:

*Births*
- Consular Births, 1849–1965
- UK High Commission Births, to 1981
- Marine Births, 1837–1965
- Air Births, 1947–65
- Births Abroad, from 1966

*Marriages*
- Consular Marriages, 1849–1965
- UK High Commission Marriages, to 1965
- 'Article 7' Marriages, to 1965
- Marriages Abroad, from 1966

*Deaths*
- Consular Deaths, 1849–1965
- Marine Deaths, 1837–1965
- UK High Commission Deaths, to 1965
- Air Deaths, 1947–65
- Deaths Abroad, from 1966

These records are often described as the births, marriages and deaths of British citizens while overseas. However, they also contain the names of many foreign nationals who were born or died on board British-registered ships. The certificates supplied by the General Register Office are in the same format as those for births, marriages and deaths in England and Wales, and the information they contain will vary, depending on the original source. This source is not always a birth, marriage or death register, and may contain information not included in the certified copy.

Unfortunately, there is no way that you can see this source, since the law requires that information may only be given in the form of a certified copy, and there is no provision for including details not covered by any of the headings on the certificate form. This is most likely to happen in the case of a birth or death at sea, when the event is recorded in the ship's log. If you know the name of the ship and the date of the event, you may be able to locate the log and view the entry for the date concerned. This is not always a straightforward business in the case of merchant shipping, and in general you will stand a better chance with twentieth-century logs than earlier ones.

Some marriages, known as 'Article 7' marriages from a clause in the 1970 Foreign Marriage Order, are marriages registered in foreign countries, where a copy of the certificate has been lodged with the British consulate, and transmitted to the Registrar General. This is done by some couples so that a replacement certified copy might easily be obtained in future, without having to apply to the registration service of the country concerned. However, since 1970 there are certain countries where there is no provision for any form of consular or High Commission registration to be made. These are known as 'No provision' countries, and they include Australia, New Zealand, Canada, South Africa, Zimbabwe and the Falkland Islands.

Events in foreign countries might be registered with a British consulate, but in colonies of the British Empire the only registration would be in the colony itself. After a colony gained its independence events might be transmitted to the Registrar General through the High Commission in that country.

Deaths on British-registered hovercraft and off-shore installations are included in Marine Deaths, to 1965, and Air Deaths include missing persons defined as 'persons with respect to whom there are reasonable grounds for believing that they have died in consequence of an accident to an aircraft registered in Great Britain and Northern Ireland'. From 1966 there are no longer separate indexes, only combined 'Overseas' indexes for births, marriages and deaths.

The 1836 Registration Act made provision for details of births and deaths at sea to be delivered to the local registrar when the vessel arrived in port. The details were then to be forwarded by post to the Registrar General. A further Act in 1874 required that deaths at sea

*New Cunard steamship, 1853.* (W and R Chambers (eds), *Chambers Information for the People,* 1853)

should be sent to the Registrar General of Shipping and Seamen in the case of merchant shipping, and to the Admiralty for Royal Navy vessels. They were then to be sent to the Registrar General for inclusion in the Marine Registers. Although the wording was identical in the two clauses of the Act, in practice only deaths on merchant vessels found their way into the indexes for several decades of its operation.

Although the General Register Office's collection of overseas records is a substantial one, there are many other places where you may find the record of a birth, marriage or death overseas. The National Archives holds many of these, and some of them duplicate the entries in the General Register Office registers. Since the General Register Office records require you to buy an expensive certified copy, it is worth checking this collection first, since a copy will be cheaper than the cost of a General Register Office certified copy. The main collection is in record series RG 32 to RG 36, digitised and indexed online at www.BMDregisters.co.uk (pay per view) or www.thegenealogist. co.uk (by subscription). A few births and deaths at sea are included in some of these overseas collections, and there are further collections of births and deaths at sea in several series of records collected by the Board of Trade.

These records comprise registers from British consulates, embassies and legations, and from some British churches abroad. There are also large collections of certificates issued by foreign registration authorities, in the local languages. Some of the records are documents sent by individuals to be lodged with the Registrar General, some items relating to the Channel Islands, and a return of births on Lundy Island, for which no provision had been made in the first Registration Acts. Unlike the General Register Office collection, these records list many events from British protectorates in Africa and Asia.

A further set of registers forms part of the Foreign Office collection, and a smaller number of registers can be found in other record series. There is a list of overseas registers in Amanda Bevan's *Tracing Your Ancestors in The National Archives: The Website and Beyond* (2006). Some of the registers in the Foreign Office collections are indexed at www.familysearch.org, but at the time of writing are difficult to search as a collection because they are listed in the general collections of births, baptisms, marriages, deaths and burials for Britain.

There are a number of files in the Foreign Office collections relating to British cemeteries abroad, and while most of them contain only correspondence about the management of the cemeteries, there are occasional references to the burials themselves. For example, a file on the British Cemetery in Naples dated 1845–54 includes details of some burials there in 1848–9 and 1852–3. There is also a volume of deaths of emigrants at sea 1847–54, containing several hundred entries, also indicating whether they were English, Scotch or Irish.

The National Archives holds a small number of birth, marriage and death records from India, mostly from those parts of India known as the Princely States. These were technically independent states and not part of the British Empire, and when India and Pakistan gained their independence there was some confusion as to the status of these records, which may explain why they were not deposited in the British Library.

The India Office Collection at the British Library is the archive of the British administration in India, including records of births, marriages and deaths, mainly in the form of church registers, known as the Ecclesiastical Returns. There is some overlap with the Indian records at The National Archives. Some of these records can be searched online at indiafamily.bl.uk but there is a great deal more material on site at the British Library.

Many of the records have also been microfilmed and some are indexed at www.familysearch.org. A collection of the microfilms is also held at the Family History Library in Salt Lake City, and copies can be ordered, for a fee, at Family History Centers all over the world. British India was divided into three Presidencies, Bengal, Bombay and Madras. There are separate indexes for each of them, so if you do not know where in India your ancestors lived, you will need to search all three. Bengal was the largest of them by a long way, so this is usually the best place to start. The records begin in the earliest days of the East India Company in the seventeenth century, and continue until 1948. They are known to be incomplete, and they relate mainly to British and European settlers. You should also bear in mind that although the collection is known as the India Office Records, the area covered is much larger than modern-day India, taking in Pakistan, Bangladesh and Burma.

A further important collection of records is held at the London Metropolitan Archives, in the archives of the Bishop of London, and of the Bishop of Gibraltar and his successors. These are records from Anglican churches overseas, mainly in Europe, and date mainly from the eighteenth and nineteenth centuries. The Bishop of London had responsibility for Anglican chaplaincies abroad where no local bishop had been appointed. When the Diocese of Gibraltar was formed in 1842 it took over responsibility for southern Europe, and the Bishop of London relinquished all overseas jurisdiction, on the formation of the single diocese of Gibraltar in Europe. Not all of the registers of these Anglican chaplaincies are deposited in the Bishop of London's collection at the London Metropolitan Archives; some are retained in the countries of origin. The collection at the London Metropolitan Archives also includes the Bishop of London's 'International Memoranda', 1816 to 1924. These are registrations of baptisms, marriages and burials abroad, mainly from British Embassy chapels. There is also a collection of original baptism, marriage and burial certificates sent to the Bishop of London for registration, and a memorandum book kept by the Bishop of Gibraltar from 1921 to 1969.

Many of the records in the London Metropolitan Archives collections, which were formerly held at Guildhall Library, are indexed at www.familysearch.org. There is a comprehensive guide to these collections and other records in the Guildhall Library's *The British Overseas: A Guide to Records of their Births, Baptisms, Marriages, Deaths and Burials Available in the United Kingdom* (3rd edn, 1994). Since this book was published many of the addresses listed in it have changed, but it remains an excellent guide to an extremely complex set of records.

## Chapter 9

# MILITARY SOURCES:
## 'The Registration of Deaths, Births and Marriages Among Officers and Soldiers of Her Majesty's Land Forces'

T he origins of the British Army can be traced back to the period immediately following the Restoration when Charles II founded England's first standing army – a force that, for the first time, would exist in times of peace as well as war.

There was some initial resistance to the idea of maintaining a full-time military force, as a result of which the English Army didn't become fully established until the reign of William III, when a series of foreign wars was fought and the need for a larger, regular army began to become clear. In 1707, the Union of England and Scotland led to the amalgamation of the two nations' armies and it was also around this time that British interests overseas rapidly expanded.

Along with this expansion came the growing need to defend these interests and, increasingly, regiments of the British Army were stationed overseas for long periods. For young single men this could be seen as an opportunity for adventure and a means of escaping the poverty facing them at home, but for married men being away from their families for years at a time presented some genuine difficulties. It wasn't until the late nineteenth century that the Army introduced a married roll and started to pay a small allowance for families. From the late 1880s, soldiers' wives started to be listed on the regimental muster rolls, together with the numbers (but not names) of the couple's children, but each regiment had a limited number of places available on the married establishment so not all married couples were entitled to the allowance.

The choice facing soldiers and their families for the first 200 years of the Army's existence was therefore quite simple: the families could stay at home and face an uncertain future or they could take their chances and, at their own expense, follow their husbands wherever the regiment took them. Most chose the latter course, although they still had to go through a 'ballot' to be allowed to accompany their husbands.

Many of the wives found work cooking and cleaning for the regiment in a semi-official role, but for others it was a matter of eking out a living on their husbands' meagre pay. And as there was no official accommodation for wives and families in the barracks, the best they could hope for was a curtained-off 'room' at one end of the living quarters.

The very presence of soldiers' wives in and around the barracks naturally led to births of children, and the regiments eventually took on the responsibility of recording these births and the all-too frequent deaths of the infants who were born in the appalling conditions. Some of the men met and married women on their travels – often the daughters of fellow soldiers, but sometimes local women, many of whom were left behind when the regiment moved on.

The British Army's records of these life events, known collectively as the Regimental Registers, include entries from as early as 1761, nearly eighty years before the start of civil registration in England and Wales. The registers are now held by the General Register Office and are used to issue official certificates of births, marriages and deaths.

There are in fact very few eighteenth-century births in the registers – the vast majority date from the early 1800s onwards and continue right up to 1924. The records include births and baptisms that took place while the regiments were stationed at home (in England, Wales, Scotland and Ireland), as well as thousands from far-flung parts of the British Empire. In many cases, the 'home' births were also registered with the local authorities but sometimes the Army certificate is the only record of the birth.

*Extract from the Registry of Marriages and Baptisms of the Royal Artillery detailing records of the family of Frank Spohr Cooper.* (The National Archives WO97/2557)

The Regimental Registers of births and baptisms have been well indexed and the indexes themselves are quite informative, giving the first name and any middle initials of the child, the place of birth (usually where the regiment was stationed), the year of birth, the name of the regiment and a unique reference consisting of a volume and page number which are used to identify each individual entry.

Unfortunately, the Regimental Registers of marriages and deaths are not fully indexed. A card index held by the General Register Office and not publicly accessible is the only comprehensive means of access to the many thousands of entries recorded in the registers.

In addition to the Regimental Registers, a separate series of Army registers was started at the end of the eighteenth century. These are the Chaplains' Returns which run from 1796 to 1880.

The Army Chaplains' Department was formed by Royal Warrant in 1796 to formalise the previously haphazard method of appointing chaplains to army regiments. The records kept by the chaplains also found their way into the hands of the General Register Office and are accompanied by an excellent set of indexes. Like the larger collection of Regimental Registers, the Chaplains' Returns include records of events occurring both at home and abroad. There is a degree of duplication between the two sets of records.

The Chaplains' Returns are continued from 1881 (for overseas events only) as the General Register Office's series of Army Returns which themselves run until 1965.

The General Register Office also holds indexes to the deaths of British soldiers occurring in the South African (or Boer) wars (1899–1902), the First World War (1914–21) and the Second World War (1939–45). The records of the two world wars include deaths occurring some years after the conflicts due to wounds or illnesses incurred as a result of military action. The records of the officers and men who died in the First World War are vast, recording over 800,000 names. The indexes alone comprise thirteen large volumes.

The British Army has always attracted men from all parts of the British Isles and a disproportionately large number of soldiers from Ireland and Scotland joined the ranks. The records of these men, their marriages and deaths, and the births of their children are included in the General Register Office's Army registers. This is an important

*British soldiers at dinner in camp, Aldershot, 1889.* (The National Archives COPY 1/397)

point to remember for those seeking records of their Scottish and Irish military ancestors.

While these registers found their way into the hands of the General Register Office for England and Wales, the main series of War Office records is held by The National Archives. It is a huge collection of records, comprising 408 distinct series, many of which are of enormous interest to family historians. Army service records and muster rolls, which include important biographical information on individual soldiers, will be covered later (see Chapter 15), but The National Archives also holds a large number of registers of baptisms, marriages and burials, compiled by a wide range of military institutions, under the auspices of the War Office.

For the Royal Artillery there are registers of baptisms and marriages as well as registers of deceased soldiers; there is a register of deaths at the Royal Chelsea Hospital covering the years 1795–1816; and a whole series of miscellaneous registers of baptisms, marriages and burials from a variety of garrison churches at home and abroad.

Under the terms of the Test and Corporation Acts (see Chapter 7) all prospective Army officers had to provide proof of baptism in the Church of England. There are two separate collections of the certificates submitted to the War Office, one dating from 1777–1892 and the other (which also includes records of marriages and burials) covering the years 1755–1908, which have been extracted from a variety of files and are fully indexed.

A further set of registers kept by the Chelsea Hospital is also held by The National Archives among the records of the Registrar General. These registers start as early as 1691 and the records of burials continue (with some gaps) right up to the middle of the nineteenth century.

Also among the records collected by the General Register Office but now held by The National Archives (in the Miscellaneous Foreign Death Returns) is an incomplete set of twenty-six registers relating to British military deaths in French and Belgian Field Hospitals during the First World War.

The extensive records of the British in India, held by the British Library, include many military records alongside those of the civilian population.

The role played by the Royal Navy in the story of the British Empire can't be overestimated but since married women didn't, as a rule, follow their seafaring husbands on their journeys around the world, the records of naval births, marriages and deaths are some-what thin on the ground compared with their Army equivalents. Most of the surviving records relate to hospitals and barracks in England. The National Archives, for example, hold a major series of registers from the Royal Naval Hospital at Greenwich. The earliest entries in these registers date from 1705 and they run (again with some gaps) up to 1857.

The General Register Office holds records of naval deaths in the two world wars; earlier surviving registers can be found among the records of the Admiralty at The National Archives. These include the registers of the Naval Hospital at Haslar (Portsmouth)

*Greenwich Pensioners.* (Printed ephemera – authors' collection)

and those of the Church at Sheerness Dockyard, the latter starting as early as 1688. There are also records from as far afield as Bermuda, Malta, Singapore and Londonderry.

The Royal Marines are well represented in the Admiralty's records, particularly the Chatham and Plymouth divisions. Chatham is covered by registers dating from 1830–1913, while the records for Plymouth start even earlier, in 1810, and continue (with gaps) up to 1920. There are also baptisms for the Marines' Woolwich Division, from the Depots at Walmer, Eastney and Deal and from the Depot Church at Canterbury.

Another series of registers records the deaths of British prisoners during the Napoleonic Wars in Antigua, Jamaica, America and France. There is even a register of baptisms from the 'Electrical and Wireless School, RAF Flowerdown and RAF Worthy Down, Winchester, Hampshire', dating from 1921–50. The Admiralty's records are a treasure trove including more than 200 registers which, in one way or another, record the births, marriages and deaths of naval personnel.

Records of British military and naval personnel can be found dotted throughout the collections of The National Archives, often mixed in with records of civilians. Of particular interest are those of the Colonial and Foreign Offices. The War Office and the Admiralty had close dealings with the other branches of the British Government all around the world and baptism, marriage and burial registers can crop up almost anywhere. Many of the registers held by The National Archives include very recent entries and some collections are still being added to today.

From 1966 onwards, the records of all military registrations held by the General Register Office are included in the all-encompassing indexes to overseas events.

For nearly 300 years, the task of defending the vast British Empire took thousands of ordinary British men (and some women) to the furthest flung corners of the earth. Collecting and recording the records of our military and naval ancestors has never been an exact science and the surviving documents are some distance from representing a comprehensive record of their lives.

In the early years, keeping such records wouldn't have been seen as a priority but as time progressed the record-keeping systems became increasingly efficient. By the end of the nineteenth century there was an excellent record of the men and women who served Queen and Country in the 'empire on which the sun never set'.

*Chapter 10*

# SCOTLAND:
## 'A Complete and Uniform System of Registration of Births, Deaths, and Marriages Should be Established and Maintained in Scotland'

The history of the recording of births, marriages and deaths in Scotland is similar to England, but there are some important differences. Church records date back to the sixteenth century, and a system of civil registration was introduced later, as in England. The Church of Scotland was, and is, the national church, but without the established status of the Church of England and the Church in Wales. Another important difference is that there are no bishops in the Church of Scotland, therefore there are no Bishop's Transcripts. Outside the Church of Scotland there are many Protestant Non-conformist denominations, as there are in England, as well as Roman Catholic and Jewish congregations.

Civil registration was introduced in Scotland in 1855, nearly two decades later than in England and Wales, but far more information is recorded in these records, which goes some way towards compensating for the later start. Another advantage of the Scottish system of registration is that the registers themselves can be viewed, and uncertified copies made, unlike the more restrictive legislation in England and Wales.

The earliest surviving parish register in Scotland is dated 1538 but unfortunately most Scottish registers start much later, and there are many gaps in coverage. There were no Scottish equivalents of

Hardwicke's or Rose's Acts, so the information contained in the registers is variable, where there is a register at all. Burial registers are particularly scarce, although there are some notable exceptions – the burial registers for Glasgow Cathedral, for example, are unusually detailed.

When a funeral took place the coffin would be covered with a 'mort-cloth' and where there is no surviving burial register there may be a record of the hiring of this cloth. Baptism and marriage records survive in greater numbers, and although they resemble pre-Hardwicke and pre-Rose English parish registers, there are some differences.

One of the great advantages of Scottish records is that a woman's maiden surname does not disappear altogether when she marries, even in early records. In some cases women might revert to their maiden names entirely on widowhood. A birth or baptism record where the parents have different surnames is a reflection of this custom, and does not mean that they were not married, although a baptism entry might refer to a couple as Peter Carrick and his wife, Janet Rankin. Marriage records also need to be treated with care, since they may be records of the proclamation – similar to banns in England – rather than the marriage ceremony itself. This is because Scots marriage law is very different from its English counterpart, and until as recently as 1916 a public declaration before witnesses, and without preliminaries or any religious ceremony, could constitute a binding marriage.

All surviving Church of Scotland registers are held by the General Register Office for Scotland, now part of the National Records of Scotland. They are known as the Old Parish Registers, and they have all been digitised and indexed. They can be searched online at www.scotlandspeople.gov.uk on a pay-per-view basis, or on site at the ScotlandsPeople Centre in Edinburgh. A fee is payable for a day's research there, but this entitles you to unlimited access to all the records, with additional charges only for printing images or downloading them onto a portable memory device.

Records of other churches may be harder to find, but many of them were collected by the National Archives of Scotland, also now part of the National Records of Scotland. So far only Roman Catholic registers are available on the ScotlandsPeople website.

When a family disappears from the records of a parish in England, it usually indicates that they have moved away, but in Scotland there could be a different explanation. Scottish church history can be very complicated, and the family might not have moved at all, instead the minister and the entire congregation could have changed their allegiance and left the Church of Scotland. This is a particularly common occurrence in the 'Great Disruption' of 1843 when hundreds of ministers left the Church of Scotland to form the Free Church of Scotland, often taking their parishioners with them. Not all surviving non-Church of Scotland registers are held in Edinburgh; many are held in local archives.

Civil registration finally came to Scotland on 1 January 1855, and its records are known as Statutory Registers. Like the Old Parish Registers, they are part of the collection of Registrar General's records which form part of the National Records of Scotland. Scotland was divided into registration districts, generally based on single parishes, most Scottish parishes being much larger than English ones. The registrars were often schoolmasters or sessions clerks.

One of the most significant features of the Scottish Act of 1854 was that it did not restrict access to certified copies like the 1836 Act for England and Wales. As a result, it has always been possible for researchers to view the registers held in Edinburgh, and for uncertified extracts to be made from them. The original indexes were in the bound volumes, then on microfiche, and now in digitised format. They can also be searched at the ScotlandsPeople Centre or online at www.scotlandspeople.gov.uk.

In the first year of operation an astonishing amount of information was gathered for each birth, marriage and death registration. So much, in fact, that it proved unsustainable, and in 1856 was scaled down considerably, with some elements restored in 1861. The 1855 certificates are exceptionally useful, but even when they were at their least informative from 1856 to 1860 Scottish certificates still contain more detail than their equivalents in England and Wales.

If you are lucky, one of your Scottish ancestors will have been born, or married or died in 1855 and you will have the benefit of one of these amazing certificates. If not, it is well worth checking to see if someone to whom they were related did so. The extra information appearing only on 1855 certificates is as follows:

*Births*
Information on the child's siblings, date and place of birth of both parents. The date and place of their marriage was dropped from 1856–60, and then restored.

*Marriages*
Birthplaces and number of former marriages of both parties (plus the number of children by those marriages). Birthplaces and previous marriage details were dropped after 1855, but the former was restored from 1972.

*Deaths*
Birthplace of the deceased, names and years of birth of their children, plus years of death for any that pre-deceased the parent, place of burial and the name of the undertaker. Details of birthplace and of children were dropped from 1856, but burial information continued until 1860.

There are slightly different interfaces for searching the records at the ScotlandsPeople Centre and online, but the main difference is that not all of the registers can be viewed on the ScotlandsPeople website. Although all births, marriages and deaths can be seen at the ScotlandsPeople Centre as soon as they are available, there is a time restriction on those you can view online. The limits are 100 years for births, 75 years for marriages and 50 years for deaths, so every January another year's worth of births, marriages and deaths is released on the site. The indexes are available online, so that you can identify the entry you need and order an Official Extract in the same way that you would order a certificate in England and Wales. However, although the recent records can be seen on site in Edinburgh, you can only make notes of the contents, as the printing and downloading functions are disabled for the records within the same 100, 75 and 50-year limits as those online.

The extra information on Scottish certificates is not only extremely useful, but also means that you can use different research strategies that are not possible with English and Welsh records. As with the Old Parish Registers, the Statutory Registers continue to record more information about women and their maiden names.

Scottish birth certificates give the child's surname as well as the forename(s), which was not the case in England and Wales until 1969. The date and place of birth, the names of both parents and the father's occupation are also given. But unlike English and Welsh certificates, the time of birth is always shown, and from 1861 onwards the date and place of the parents' marriage is also shown, assuming of course that it has actually taken place. Where a child was born to unmarried parents, the word 'illegitimate' was written above the child's name until 1919. If both parents are named on the certificate then the child's name will include both surnames, and the birth will also be indexed under both surnames. There may be extra details as in the illegitimate birth of Robert McIntyre or Collins, born in 1874, where his mother is described as 'Jane McIntyre … widow of Patrick Collins, engineer, who died in March 1871'.

Marriage certificates in Scotland are a treasure trove of information for the genealogist. Scots marriage law has always been much less restrictive than English marriage law in a number of respects. Even today the age at which a person can marry in Scotland without parental consent is 16, while in England and Wales the age of majority was 21 until 1969 and is now 18. This accounts for the popularity of Gretna Green as a place of marriage for English runaways, since it is the first place over the border on one of the main routes from England into Scotland. Of course anywhere in Scotland would do just as well (Lamberton Toll fulfilled a similar role on the main road into Scotland on the east) and since Gretna might be the first place the parents of the eloping pair would look, a smart couple might be well advised to proceed a little further north.

Most marriages in the nineteenth century and much of the twentieth took the form of a religious ceremony of some kind, but need not be in a church or chapel. There was no requirement for either the place of marriage or the celebrant to be licensed, and there was no equivalent in Scotland of the English registrar of marriages or of the register

*A Scottish wedding, 1884.* (*Girls Own Paper*, 1884)

office wedding until 1939. The marriage was officially registered by notifying the local registrar and the entry in the marriage register would be completed. A couple could also marry without any religious ceremony by making a declaration in front of witnesses, and if they wanted to register their marriage they needed first to obtain a warrant from the local Sheriff Substitute, and then to proceed to the registry office where their marriage would be entered in the register. These are known as marriages by declaration.

There was also a third and much rarer kind of marriage, by 'custom and repute'. This would occur where a couple had lived together for a number of years as man and wife, and were known by friends and neighbours as a married couple; simple co-habitation was not enough. By definition these unions were not registered, and there would be a written record only if a court had been required to pass judgement on the legality of such a marriage.

The entry in the Statutory marriage register shows the date and place of the marriage, and the religious denomination, if any. The full names of both parties are given, and if the couple were cousins this is indicated. Although cousin marriages are fairly unusual, this is a helpful piece of information because it is not always easy to work out from the names alone, especially in those parts of Scotland where many people share the same surname, whether or not they are related. The full names, ages, marital status, addresses and occupations of both parties are given, just as they would be south of the border. But the names of all four parents are also listed, stating if they were deceased at the time of the wedding. The maiden names of the mothers are also given, and better still, if a mother had been married more than once, all of her married names will be shown. This could be the first indication of such a re-marriage, which might otherwise be hard to find. The signatures of at least two witnesses and of the officiating minister are listed, and finally the date of registration and the signature of the registrar.

Unlike their English counterparts, Scottish death certificates contain enough information to make them an integral part of the research process. The death certificates of married people, widows and widowers also list the names of their current and any previous spouses. In common with birth entries, the actual time of death is also recorded, and if the deceased's usual address is different from the place of death, this is shown too. The later start date of Scottish registration is more than compensated for by the fact that death certificates always give the names of the parents of the deceased, regardless of their age at death. So the death of an elderly ancestor in the early years of registration will give the names of parents who were born in the early years of the eighteenth century, and of course the maiden name of the mother is included. As with all such cases, the information is only ever as good as the person who supplied it and a man registering the death of an elderly grandparent may not be fully aware of the correct details.

Another feature of the death indexes is that married women and widows are indexed under both their maiden and married surnames. This means that it is often easier to find the records of the women in your family than of the men, because if you already know both names

**1942. DEATHS in the District of Newington in the City of Edinburgh**

| No. (1.) | Name and Surname. Rank or Profession, and whether Single, Married, or Widowed. | When and Where Died. (2.) | Sex. (3.) | Age. (4.) | Name, Surname, and Rank or Profession of Father. Name, and Maiden Surname of Mother. (5.) | Cause of Death, Duration of Disease, and Medical Attendant by whom certified. (6.) | Signature and Qualification of Informant, and Residence, if out of the House in which the Death occurred. (7.) | When and Where Registered, and Signature of Registrar. (8.) |
|---|---|---|---|---|---|---|---|---|
| 154 | | | M | | | | | 1942. |
| 155 | Samuel Christie Annal | 1942. | M | 59 years | | | | 1942. |
| 156 | | 1942. | M | 3 months | | | | 1942. |

*Death certificate of Samuel Christie Annal, 1942. (General Record Office (Scotland) Ref: 685/06 0155)*

you can look for a pair of index entries with the same reference, rather like searching for a marriage in England or Wales. So even if your female ancestor had a very common name like Janet Brown or Mary Fraser, you will be able to identify her death more easily than that of her husband, who only has one surname. Another benefit of the cross-referencing of women's names is that it makes it easier to trace forwards, since daughters do not effectively disappear from view when they marry if you do not know the name of the husband.

When it is found that there is an error in a register entry, or there is additional information to add, the entry itself is not amended as in England and Wales, but a separate record is made in the Register of Corrected Entries and a note of this made on the entry itself. This might be the addition of a father's name to the birth entry of a child born out of wedlock, following a court case establishing paternity, or on a death entry it may be the result of an inquiry into a sudden death by the Procurator Fiscal, the equivalent of a coroner's inquest in England and Wales. There may be simple corrections, as in the death of William Carden who died on 4 February 1904 in Hamilton Poorhouse. His death entry describes him as aged 63, the widower of Ann Warnock, but on 12 February there is a correction to the effect that he was 56, not 63, information supplied by the very much alive Ann Warnock, also causing his status to be changed from 'widower' to 'husband'.

When researching Scottish family history it is useful to know about the customary naming pattern that was widely followed. The first son in the family would be named after his paternal grandfather, the second after the maternal grandfather, the third after his own father and any further sons might be given the names of their paternal and maternal uncles. Daughters were named in the same way, but starting with the maternal grandmother, then the paternal grandmother, and so on.

This has the advantage that you can often work out names that were likely to have been used for 'missing' family members, for example, children who were born and died between census years. The disadvantage of the naming pattern is that it can result in a number of people in a family with exactly the same name; if a man had several sons, they would all call their first son the name of their father, resulting in a number of identically named men who were first cousins. This is confusing enough for the genealogist, and it could cause problems for the families themselves too. One of the ways of dealing with this was the creative use of diminutives and nicknames, and another was the addition of family surnames as middle names for both sexes.

The naming pattern was not strictly followed by every family, although it was very widespread. A variation was the use of feminised versions of boys' names for daughters, perhaps when the family had given up on ever producing a son. This was usually achieved by adding the suffix –ina to a masculine name. Some of the results were more successful than others, like Thomasina and Georgina, which are names in their own right, but less elegant names like Hughina and Andrewina were surprisingly popular.

Scotland also has its equivalent of the Miscellaneous Overseas Registers collection, known as the Minor Records. These are:

- Marine registers, from 1855
- Foreign returns, 1860–1965
- Service returns, from 1881
- High Commission returns, from 1964
- Consular returns, from 1914
- Air register, from 1948
- War deaths, 1899–1902, 1914–18 and 1939–45

These should contain births, marriages and deaths overseas or at sea of people of Scottish birth or parentage. However, assigning records to the correct Registrar General when they were received from overseas is not an exact science. If the relevant details were not available this might be a matter of guesswork. You should therefore also search the Miscellaneous Overseas collection for England and Wales for records of Scottish people abroad. It is also possible for the same event to be recorded in more than one place; the death of Thomas Cross, a merchant seaman normally resident in Glasgow, and who died at sea in 1917, is recorded in the Marine Register in Scotland, and also in the equivalent register in England and Wales.

*Chapter 11*

# IRELAND:
## 'A Complete System of Registration of Births and Deaths Should be Established in Ireland'

A basic understanding of the religious and political history of Ireland is essential to anyone wishing to research the turbulent history of the island, through its surviving records.

For more than a hundred years, from 1801 until the creation of the Free State in 1922, Ireland was an integral part of the British Isles. The island had been effectively ruled by the English since the mid-1500s but, like Scotland, had always retained its own legal system and a degree of self-government.

The English Protestant Reformation had little or no impact on the vast majority of the population in Ireland who continued to follow the Roman Catholic faith. The 1831 census revealed that 80 per cent of Ireland's population were Catholics, compared to just 11 per cent who were members of the Anglican Church of Ireland. The remainder were followers of a variety of Protestant denominations, with the Presbyterians representing the largest single group. This devotion to the old faith was in spite of constant persecution of Catholics who were effectively removed from all positions of political power and treated as second-class citizens.

Towards the end of the eighteenth century, the authority of the Anglo-Irish rulers (the so-called Protestant Ascendancy) was challenged by an alliance of Catholics and Presbyterians known as the Society of United Irishmen. The Society sought greater democracy and one of its initial aims was Catholic Emancipation. The situation came to a head in May 1798 when an attempt was made to overthrow the Irish Government by armed force. Eventually, after some intense fighting, the rebellion was suppressed and political union with England, Wales and Scotland soon followed. The Act of Union came into effect on 1 January 1801, uniting the Kingdoms of Great Britain and Ireland.

The Church of Ireland had been established in 1536 by an Act of Parliament and in 1560 was confirmed as the Church of State. For more than 300 years, the Church of Ireland continued in this role, acting as the State's official registrar, until 1869 when the Irish Church Act decreed that all religions were to be equally recognised in Ireland, and Church and State were effectively separated.

The Church of Ireland parishes that were set up by the 1536 Act adopted a very similar record-keeping system to that used in England and Wales. Each parish kept records of baptisms, marriages and burials, which, from 1807 onwards were usually entered in pre-printed registers, similar in format to those that were later introduced in England and Wales by Rose's Act. Bishop's Transcripts were required to be kept from 1634.

The earliest known Church of Ireland parish register dates from 1619, recording events from the parish of St John's, Dublin. The majority of the surviving Anglican registers, however, date from the mid-eighteenth century and most are now held by the Church of Ireland's Representative Church Body Library (RCBL), Braemor Park, Churchtown, Dublin 14 (www.ireland.anglican.org/library).

In the earliest registers, records of baptisms rarely provide more than the date of baptism, and the names of the child and its parents. Occasionally, details of the father's occupation and the parents' residence are to be found. Marriages usually record just the date of the wedding and the names of the bride and groom. From 1845, with the introduction of State registration of non-Catholic marriages, Church of Ireland marriage registers record a vastly increased amount of detail. Most entries in Church of Ireland burial registers consist of no more than the date of burial and the name of the deceased. However, it's not uncommon to find the age of the deceased recorded, along with information about the person's residence.

The Penal Laws introduced in 1695 led to many years of relentless persecution of Roman Catholics. Not only were Catholics prevented from holding public office or voting, they were also denied the right to own land. As in England, the situation gradually relaxed and by the middle of the eighteenth century some Catholic registers begin to appear, mostly from urban areas – the registers of St Catherine's, for example, start as early as 1740. However, it wasn't until the Catholic Emancipation Act of 1829 that Roman Catholics felt free to worship openly and it became the rule rather than the exception for Catholic parishes to keep their own records. There are therefore very few Irish Catholic registers dating from before the 1820s.

Records of baptisms often include the names of the child's sponsors (godparents) and record the mother's maiden surname as a matter of course. Catholic marriages will sometimes indicate the degree of relationship, if any, between the bride and the groom. The bride and groom's fathers' names are recorded along with their occupations and the signatures of two witnesses who are usually close relatives – although the relationship is not stated. Burial records are few and far between.

A number of Catholic registers, particularly those from the rural Irish-speaking parts of the country, were written in Latin. This shouldn't prove too big an obstacle for modern researchers as the entries were written in a highly formulaic style and the English spellings of surnames and place names were retained. Most original Catholic registers are still held locally but many have been micro-filmed and copies (up to 1880) are held at the National Library of Ireland, in Dublin (www.nli.ie).

Over the years, a number of other religious groups have had significant followings in Ireland, particularly the Presbyterians. The history of Presbyterianism in Ireland can be traced back to the early 1600s when large numbers of Scots arrived in Ulster, fleeing religious persecution. By the middle of the seventeenth century there were more than 100,000 Presbyterians in Ireland, mainly, but not exclusively, in the north of the island. The earliest known Presbyterian register (for Antrim) dates from around this period, with entries starting in 1674.

In 1782 Presbyterian marriages were formally legalised and in 1819 Presbyterian ministers were ordered to keep registers of baptisms and marriages; the majority of surviving Presbyterian registers start during the 1820s.

As with Roman Catholic registers, the originals tend to remain in the custody of the churches but, again, microfilm copies are available. The Public Record Office of Northern Ireland in Belfast (www.proni. gov.uk) has copies of the vast majority of the Presbyterian registers for the six counties that make up Northern Ireland (Down, Antrim, Armagh, Londonderry, Fermanagh and Tyrone), as well as many from the counties of Donegal, Cavan and Monaghan.

Quakers, Methodists, Baptists, Congregationalists and many other religious groups also left their mark in Ireland and, in the main, their surviving records are still held by the relevant religious communities, although microfilm copies may be held by the National Library in Dublin or the Public Record Office of Northern Ireland. The Quakers, for example, have a large collection of records that can be seen at the Friends' Historical Library in Dublin (www.quakers-in-ireland.ie/historical-library).

Since the country's history is riddled with religious strife and political struggles, it is perhaps not surprising that the 'Troubles' have had a direct impact on the condition and survival of Ireland's historical records. In April 1922, fighting between Provisional Government troops and Irish Republican Army militants who had occupied the Four Courts building (home of the Irish Public Record Office) in Dublin resulted in the destruction of thousands of legal and religious documents, charting Ireland's history. Most of the damage was as a result of a fire, caused by a huge explosion when an ammunition store kept by the defending garrison was struck by a shell.

In 1876, an Act had been passed requiring the Church of Ireland (as the State's erstwhile official record keeper) to deposit its registers with the Public Record Office (now the National Archives of Ireland) (www.nationalarchives.ie). Ironically, as a result of this apparently forward-thinking legislation, a large number of Church of Ireland parish registers were among the irreplaceable records lost in the attack on the Four Courts.

Fortunately, an amendment to the 1876 Act, passed in 1878, allowed parishes with suitable storage conditions to retain their registers. A number of ministers also had the foresight to make copies of their registers before submitting the originals to the Public Record Office so the impact of the fire was not as great as it might have been. In an effort to prevent further catastrophes, many of the surviving registers (representing roughly 40 per cent of Anglican parishes) have now been microfilmed. The originals are spread around the country; some are in the original parishes, some have been deposited at the National Archives in Dublin or the Public Record Office of Northern Ireland and many more are held at the Church of Ireland's Representative Church Body Library.

However you look at it, the loss is a significant one, and the destruction of such a large number of 'official' State records of births, marriages and deaths has major consequences for those studying the history of Ireland and its people.

There had been an unsuccessful attempt to bring in registration of births, marriages and deaths in 1617 but it wasn't until 1845 that a form of civil registration was introduced, which at first was very limited. From 1 April 1845 all non-Roman Catholic marriages were required to be registered with the newly established civil authorities but it was nearly twenty years before the system was extended to cover all marriages, along with births and deaths. Comprehensive civil registration was introduced in Ireland on 1 January 1864 and therefore starts twenty-seven years later than in England and Wales and nine years later than in Scotland.

As with England and Wales, the administrative structure of the new registration system was based on the existing Poor Law Unions. Furthermore, the design and layout of the certificates was virtually identical to the records used in England and Wales. The indexes compiled by the Irish General Register Office also followed the same pattern, initially just giving the names and registration districts, together with a unique reference consisting of a volume and page number, but gradually more detail was added.

The oldest indexes, covering the non-Catholic marriages from 1845–63, are handwritten – all the later volumes are typed or printed. Between 1864 and 1877, there are annual indexes for each event (births, marriages and deaths) with ages at death given in the death indexes. From 1878–1902, the indexes are quarterly.

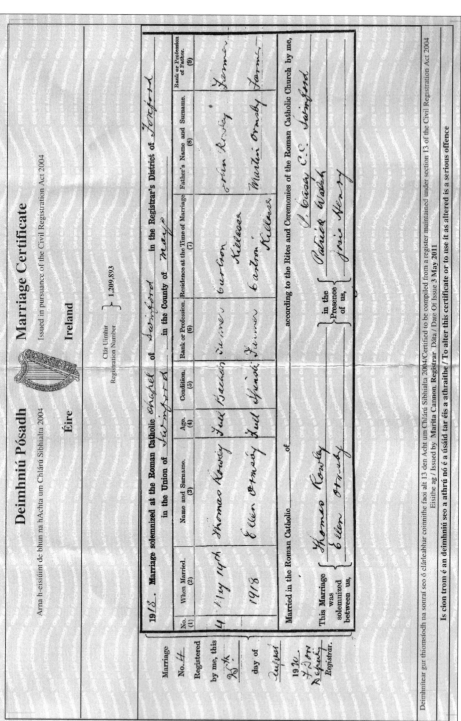

*Marriage certificate of Thomas Rowley and Ellen Ormsby, 1918.* (General Register Office Ireland, September 1920, Swineford, Vol. 4, p. 195)

From 1903–27, there are two sets of birth indexes: annual volumes that give the additional information of the date of birth and the mother's maiden name and the standard quarterly books that lack this extra detail. Throughout this period, the marriage and death indexes are arranged in quarterly volumes. From 1928, the date of birth is no longer shown in the birth indexes and all indexes are quarterly. The final change of note came in 1966 when the birth indexes once again begin to show the date of birth and the mother's maiden name; the marriage indexes record the date of the marriage and the spouse's surname and the death indexes show the date of death and the marital status of the deceased.

Of course, the biggest transformation that confronts all researchers of recent Irish history occurred in 1922 when the six counties of the north parted company with the rest of the island. The north remained part of the United Kingdom of Great Britain to form Northern Ireland, while the rest of the country became first the Irish Free State and later the Republic of Ireland. From this year onwards, the records are divided. In the Republic, the main collection of parish registers is held by the Church of Ireland's Representative Church Body Library with microfilm copies at the National Library, while the civil registration records are held by the General Register Office (www.groireland.ie). In the North, the Public Record Office of Northern Ireland and the General Register Office Northern Ireland (www.groni.gov.uk) are the relevant repositories.

The best news about Ireland's civil registration records is that they were not affected by the fire at the Four Courts building. They were held at the offices of the General Register Office and survive fully intact. With the wholesale loss of records which in other parts of Britain are fundamental to successful research, they represent the surest path back into the murky waters of Irish church records.

*Chapter 12*

# THE CHANNEL ISLANDS AND THE ISLE OF MAN

## Channel Islands

The Channel Islands are a group of islands lying in the English Channel, close to the coast of northern France. They are the last vestiges of what can be seen in some respects as the first British Empire, although the term English Empire would perhaps be more appropriate.

When William the Conqueror invaded England in 1066 he brought his French possessions with him and for the next 500 years the English Crown retained an active interest in France. The extent of English holdings across the Channel varied over the years but reached a peak in the second half of the twelfth century under King Henry II when well over half of modern France was in English hands. The last part of the French mainland to fall was the port of Calais, which was finally ceded to France in 1558.

In 1259, Henry III surrendered his claim to the lands in Normandy, but the Channel Islands were specifically excluded and have continued as possessions of the English Crown ever since.

The political status of the Channel Islands is somewhat confusing. The islands are not part of what is termed the United Kingdom but rather British Crown Dependencies and are divided into two separate Bailiwicks: the Bailiwick of Jersey and the Bailiwick of Guernsey. The latter includes, for some administrative purposes, the islands of Alderney and Sark as well as Lihou, Herm, Jethou, Burhou and Brecqhou together with a number of unoccupied islets.

## Jersey

The earliest records in the registers of Jersey's twelve ancient parishes are from the parish of St Saviour (with baptisms commencing in 1540), but none of the parishes have registers starting later than 1647 so coverage is generally good. In most cases, however, the registers are written in French until relatively recent times – this is true of all the Channel Islands' parish registers. English only became the official written language of Jersey in 1948. The good news is that women's maiden names are used as a matter of course in most records from the Channel Islands.

Jersey's parish registers are held by the Jersey Archive, Clarence Road, St Helier, Jersey JE2 4JY (www.jerseyheritage.org/research-centre/jersey-archive), along with those of a small number of Methodist, Independent and Roman Catholic churches.

Civil registration of births, marriages and deaths was introduced in Jersey in 1842. The records are held by the Office of the Superintendent Registrar, 10 Royal Square, Saint Helier, Jersey JE2 4WA.

## Guernsey

Guernsey also has some very early parish registers with several parishes boasting registers which begin in the sixteenth century – the earliest being the Town Church of the island's capital, St Peter Port, with baptisms starting in 1563. However, some of the country parishes start much later: the registers of St Sampson's begin as late as 1713.

The main repository for Guernsey Parish registers is the Priaulx Library, Candie Road, St Peter Port, Guernsey GY1 1ED (www.priaulxlibrary.co.uk).

Civil registration started in 1840 on Guernsey, but only for births and deaths; marriages weren't registered by the state until 1919. The records are held by the office of HM Greffier, Royal Court House, St Peter Port, Guernsey GY1 2PB.

## Alderney

The situation on Alderney is more complicated. There was only one parish (St Anne's) and the registers have survived (with some gaps) from the 1650s. Some later registers were lost during the German occupation in the Second World War. Civil Registration of births and deaths started in 1850 and of marriages in 1886 but there are some gaps in the records. All enquiries should be addressed to The Greffier, The Court of Alderney, Queen Elizabeth II Street, Alderney GY9 3TB (www.alderney.gov.gg/Court-of-Alderney).

All births, marriages and deaths in Alderney since 1925 are registered with the authorities in Guernsey.

*Sark*

The registers of Sark's single parish, St Peter's, start as early as 1570, but civil registration didn't begin on the island until 1925. The records are held by The Greffe, La Chasse Marette, Sark GY9 0SF.

Finding your way around the Channel Islands' records can be fraught with difficulties. Fortunately, the Channel Islands FHS (www. jerseyfamilyhistory.org) has done an enormous amount of indexing work and their resources are freely available at the Priaulx Library in Guernsey and the Jersey Archive.

## The Isle of Man

The Isle of Man is also a British Crown Dependency but has a very different history to that of the Channel Islands with its mixed Gaelic and Norse heritage. The island, situated in the Irish Sea, has been a possession of the English Crown since 1399, but, like the Channel Islands, is not part of the United Kingdom.

The Church of England is the Established Church of the Isle of Man and its registers date back to the early seventeenth century. Two of the island's ancient parishes, Ballaugh and Jurby, have registers commencing in 1607 and the vast majority start by the end of the seventeenth century. Pre-printed registers were introduced in 1849.

In 1910, all the surviving parish registers were copied by the Manx General Registry and these records, along with the original registers dating from 1849, have been microfilmed and can be seen at the Manx National Heritage Library, Douglas, Isle of Man, IM1 3LY (www. gov.im/mnh/heritage/library/nationallibrary.xml).

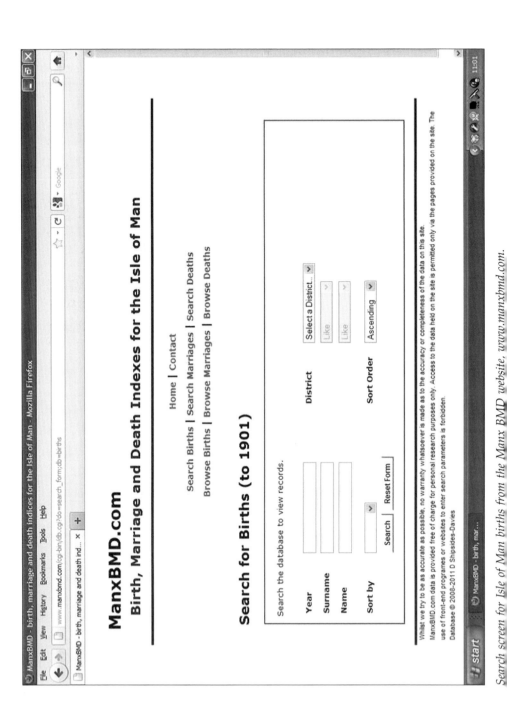

Search screen for Isle of Man births from the Manx BMD website, www.manxbmd.com.

Civil Registration was introduced in two steps. The Civil Registration Act of 1849 allowed Protestant Nonconformists and others who worshiped outside the Established Church to register their births and marriages with civil authorities – curiously the Act also allowed for retrospective registration.

Full civil registration of births and deaths followed in 1878, but marriages weren't recorded until 1884. The layout and content of Manx civil registration records is virtually identical to the records in England and Wales. Certificates are held by the Civil Registry, Deemsters Walk, Buck's Road, Douglas, IM1 3AR (www.gov.im/registries/general/civilregistry). Manxbmd (www.manxbmd.com) is an unofficial website providing access to civil registration records of births (to 1901), marriages (to 1911) and deaths (to 1911).

The Manx language was formerly spoken extensively on the island but was never used in official documents. The Isle of Man Family History Society (www.iomfhs.im) is very active and their website contains some very useful information about researching Manx family history.

*Chapter 13*

# DIVORCE:

## 'Every Person Seeking a Decree of Nullity of Marriage, or a Decree of Judicial Separation, or a Dissolution of Marriage'

Before 1858, the only way to obtain a divorce in England and Wales was through a private Act of Parliament. Not surprisingly, this was a very expensive business. This is not to say that unsatisfactory marriages did not come to an end, but that true legal divorce, allowing both parties to re-marry, was open only to a wealthy minority. Records of these divorces are held by the Parliamentary Archives.

For the rest of the population the only escape from an unhappy marriage was death, or, very rarely, annulment. An annulment would allow re-marriage, but only by establishing that the marriage had not been valid in the first place. This might be a satisfactory outcome when both parties immediately regretted their hasty marriage and wanted to be free of each other, but if one of them was opposed or there were children of the marriage there could be serious legal consequences. The other grounds for annulment were if one of the parties was coerced into the marriage, or was legally insane and unable to give consent, or was too young to marry at all. If one of the parties was already married, the marriage would be bigamous, and therefore invalid. It is still possible for a marriage to be annulled today, and, unsurprisingly, it is still rare.

For the majority of the population for whom divorce was impossible, there were alternatives. Before Hardwicke's Marriage Act, when marriage law was unclear to say the least, there were plenty of irregular marriages that could be open to legal challenge if it suited one of the parties to do so. You would also be free to re-marry if you had not seen your spouse for seven years and did not know their whereabouts, if you made a declaration to that effect. There was also the custom of the wife sale, immortalised in Thomas Hardy's the Mayor of Casterbridge. This was a fictional account, but wife sales really did take place, and were regarded in some circles as a kind of common-law divorce. They had the same legal status as common-law marriage: that is, none at all.

There was always the option of simply committing bigamy, or claiming to be husband and wife when you were not married, because one of you was still married to someone else. The first was illegal and the second immoral, in the eyes of many, but both were widely practised, sometimes to the confusion of the genealogist trying to untangle the puzzle. It is worth bearing in mind that in an age without instant communication and a mass of centralised public records it was not easy to check on the existence or validity of a marriage, and unless a deserted spouse made a complaint, or someone informed the authorities, bigamy would generally remain undetected.

Also, the lack of any means of legal divorce was nowhere near as big a problem in the nineteenth century and earlier as it would be today, for the rather grim reason that life expectancy was much shorter, and if you were dissatisfied with your spouse, you were unlikely to be shackled to them for thirty or forty years or more, since the chances of both of you living that long were not very high.

Until the mid-nineteenth century the Church of England played a significant role in the everyday lives of the population. Church courts were responsible for most of what we would now regard as family law, including the whole area of marriage law. The Church had a virtual monopoly on marriage itself from 1753–1837, when only Church of England ceremonies were legally valid. Church courts did not, however, have the authority to dissolve a marriage. They could grant a separation, known as 'a mensa et thoro', literally 'from bed and board', but this did not allow the parties to re-marry.

Two related matters were the custody of children and the rights of women to own property, over which the Church had no jurisdiction, these being matters for the civil law. A married woman had no separate legal existence, and was deemed to be one with her husband. Any property or goods that she possessed belonged to her husband as soon as she married, unless there was a marriage settlement to the contrary, or the terms of a will had stated explicitly that an inheritance was for her own personal benefit, and not for any husband she may have, or subsequently acquire.

In a marriage that was harmonious, or where the couple were so poor that there was no money to worry about, the lack of property rights for women was not an issue. In less happy circumstances, though, it could be the source of a great deal of misery and injustice. A woman who had been deserted by her husband might have great difficulty obtaining any kind of maintenance from him. Since husband and wife were a single legal entity, she could not sue him, and at that time a woman's earning power was much lower than a man's so she would be hard-pressed to make a living for herself, let alone any dependent children, if her husband left her. Nor did she have any rights over her children, and her husband, if he wished, could deny her any access to them, and no court had the authority to intervene on her behalf, no matter how violent or abusive the husband.

It was a very high-profile case that brought this to the attention of the public, and, more to the point, to the attention of the lawmakers who could do something about it. The case in question was that of Caroline Norton, a granddaughter of the playwright Sheridan, who was in a very unhappy marriage. Her husband, George Norton, from whom she was separated, refused her any financial support but she managed to earn some money by her writing. He claimed that he was entitled to this money, which indeed he was as the law stood at that time.

Being a lawyer himself, he was confident that he had the upper hand, but while Caroline had few rights and less power, she did have influence and friends in high places, notably the Prime Minister, Lord Melbourne. She used her writing skills to campaign for changes to the law so that deserted wives like herself would have some rights over

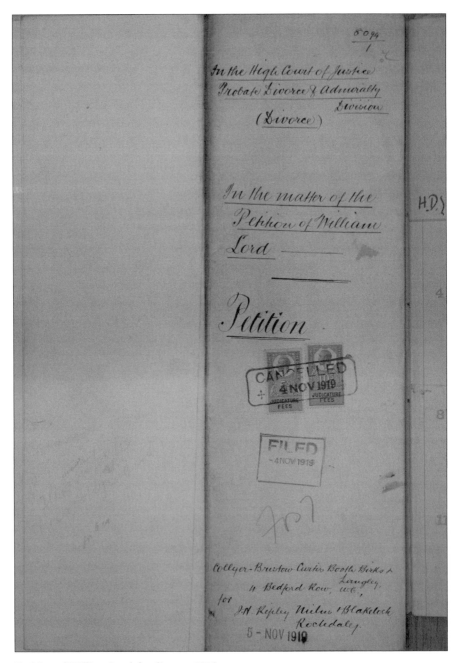

*Petition of William Lord for divorce, 1919.* (The National Archives J 77/1552/8094)

their own earnings. She also highlighted the plight of mothers who had no rights to see their own children; George had sent their three young sons away to a cousin of his in Scotland. One of the boys died while they were there so she never saw him again, and it was years before she was reunited with his brothers.

As a result of her efforts, and the willingness of Parliament to pursue the path of reform, a number of significant Acts were passed: the Infant Custody Act 1839 and eventually the Married Women's Property Acts of 1870 and 1882. But most important of all was the Divorce Act of 1857, which came into force the following year.

Despite the fact that it was still very expensive, as opposed to outrageously expensive, a good number of people took advantage of the new law and petitioned for divorce. Although women now had far more rights than previously, thanks to Caroline Norton and others, it was still easier for a man to divorce his wife than for a woman to divorce her husband. A man could divorce his wife on the grounds of adultery alone, but for a wife to divorce her husband for adultery there had to be additional grounds, such as cruelty, or adultery with a close relative of the wronged wife. An abandoned spouse could also petition for a judicial separation. This did not end the marriage, but would enable a deserted wife to seek maintenance from her husband through the courts, and absolve a deserted husband from responsibility for his wife's debts. A judicial separation might then be followed by a petition for restitution of conjugal rights. The intention of such a petition was not to force an unwilling spouse back into the bed of the petitioner, but to place on record that they refused to do so, thereby establishing the fact of desertion, which could then be used as grounds for a divorce petition.

All divorces granted in England and Wales since 1858 are recorded in the Divorce Section of the Principal Registry of the Family Division, at First Avenue House in London. Unfortunately, there are no publicly available indexes, so the only way to obtain a copy of a divorce decree is to pay for a search there, providing if possible the date of the divorce and of the marriage. The result of a successful search will be a copy of the Decree Absolute, and of the Decree Nisi if you request it. This is fine if you need legal proof that a divorce was granted, but for the family historian it is an expensive way of getting limited information about an ancestor's divorce. A Decree Absolute is simply a legal statement that the marriage was dissolved, and contains no additional information beyond the names of the parties. A Decree Nisi will show the grounds for the divorce, but with no further details. Fortunately, there are alternative ways of finding out about many divorce cases.

*P H Pridham-Wippell, divorce lawyer, from a* Vanity Fair *print, 1910.*

For the first seven decades after the passing of the Divorce Act the files are held in The National Archives at Kew, and they are indexed by name in the online catalogue. The files have been weeded, so they do not contain every document involved in each case, but they will include the petition, the response, any relevant birth or marriage certificates and from about 1870 copies of the decrees. The records also include petitions for judicial separation, restitution of conjugal rights and for annulment. Additionally, they record petitions that were unsuccessful. The petitioner might have failed to prove their case, or the parties may have been reconciled, or one of them died before the divorce was finalised.

Until 1928 all divorces were granted in the Principal Registry, but after that date other courts were empowered to grant divorces. The National Archives only holds files for cases heard at the Principal Registry, which for the period 1928–38 is about 80 per cent of the total. After 1938 the method of record keeping was changed, and only a very small sample of divorce files was kept after that, amounting to no more than a couple of dozen for each year.

But official records are not the only sources for finding out about divorces. In the nineteenth century, in particular, divorces were newsworthy, and newspaper reports from the divorce courts can be the most informative sources of all. The more recent the divorce, the less likely it is to be reported, as divorce rates have risen steadily. However, even today many cases still make the papers, usually where the parties are celebrities, but any divorce might be reported where there is an unusual feature to the case, such as protracted battles over the custody of a pet, or spectacular damage inflicted by one party on the other's cherished possessions. The *Penny Illustrated Paper*, 1861–1913, reported extensively from the divorce courts, and, as its name suggests, sketches of the warring parties sometimes appear.

If the court found that the grounds for divorce were proved, the Decree Nisi was granted, followed by a period of six weeks after which the petitioner could apply to have the divorce made final by the granting of the Decree Absolute. Once this was granted the marriage was ended and the parties were free to remarry. It was not until 1967 that divorce was permitted on the grounds of mutual consent, so if a judge discovered collusion between the parties before that date he would refuse to grant the Decree Absolute. This led to the widespread use of the legal fiction whereby a man would be 'discovered' in a hotel room with a woman who was not his wife. The wife could then obtain her divorce on the grounds of his 'adultery'.

# *Chapter 14*

# ADOPTION:
## 'The Registrar-General Shall Establish and Maintain a Register to be Called the Adopted Children Register'

## England and Wales

Legal adoption is a very modern concept with a history stretching back less than 100 years. On 1 January 1927, the General Register Office of England and Wales opened the Adopted Children Register under the terms of the 1926 Adoption Act (an Act to make provision for the adoption of infants).

Before this date, the vast majority of adoptions were informal arrangements, records of which are very rare. In a predominantly rural society with small close-knit communities, a child whose parents had died would naturally be 'adopted' by a relative, a friend or a neighbour. In many cases, the child would take on the name of the 'adoptive' family, again with no legal record.

Adoptions were often arranged by religious and charitable organisations: the name of one such organisation, Barnardo's, has become synonymous with adoption. Thomas Barnardo opened the doors of his Ragged School in 1867 and three years later his Home for Boys in the East End of London received its first 'poor and destitute' children. The various registers kept by Barnardo's (which date right back to 1867) provide a detailed record of the 350,000 boys and girls who have passed through its doors, many of whom went on to be

*Doctor Barnardo's child, 1875.* (The National Archives Image COPY 1/29)

fostered or adopted. Enquiries should be addressed to Barnardo's, Tanners Lane, Barkingside, Essex IG6 1QG.

The adoption certificate issued by the General Register Office replaces the original for all legal purposes but provides no link whatsoever to the child's original birth certificate. The General Register Office issues two types of adoption certificates: the short certificate and the full certificate.

The short certificates record the child's date of birth, place of birth, adoptive name (forename and surname) and gender. The full certificates show the same information with the addition of the names and address of the adoptive parents, the date of the adoption order and the name of the court in which the adoption was granted.

The 1926 Act ordered that the adopted child's original birth certificate should be 'marked with the word "Adopted"'. Indexes were to be created by the General Register Office, and the Act stipulated that anyone could obtain copies of adoption certificates, on the same terms as the other records held by the General Register Office.

Crucially, the 1926 Act established a system that allowed the General Register Office 'to record and make traceable the connexion between any entry in the register of births which has been marked "Adopted" ... and any corresponding entry in the Adopted Children Register'. However, it went on to state that 'such last-mentioned registers and books shall not be ... open to public inspection or search'.

The system that operated in England and Wales from 1927 until 1974 was therefore one of 'closed adoption' in which none of the parties involved (neither the adoptee nor the birth mother) had the right to access the adoption case files or to any information that would allow them to make a link between the birth family and the child.

In 1975, the law was relaxed to allow adopted persons over 18 the right to access their adoption file to gain information about their birth families. However, those adopted before 1975 are required to attend an informal meeting with an adoption counsellor.

The Adoption Contact Register was created in 1991 to enable adopted people to make contact with their birth relatives or vice versa. If both parties in an adoption case submit their details to the

Register, a match is made and contact details are made available to both parties. A separate register is maintained by the independent adoption support agency, NORCAP (www.norcap.org.uk).

The gradual trend towards 'open' adoption was further advanced in 2002 with the passing of the Adoption and Children Act which, for the first time, allowed birth mothers some (admittedly limited) access to information about their adopted children.

Certificates from the Adopted Children Register can be obtained from the Adoptions Section, Room C201, General Register Office, Trafalgar Road, Southport PR8 2HH (www.gro.gov.uk/gro/content/adoptions).

## Scotland

The Adoption of Children (Scotland) Act came into force in 1930 and was amended by a series of later Acts including the 1975 Children's Act and the Adoption and Children (Scotland) Act of 2007. An independent agency runs the 'Birthlink' register (www.birthlink.org.uk) which operates in much the same way as the Adoption Contact Register in England and Wales.

Scottish adoption records can be obtained from the General Register Office for Scotland, New Register House, Edinburgh EH1 3YT (www.gro-scotland.gov.uk).

## Northern Ireland

Legal adoption was introduced in Northern Ireland in 1931 using a very similar system to that in force in England and Wales. Anyone aged 18 or over can now get access to their adoption records.

The General Register Office for Northern Ireland operates an Adoption Contact Register.

Adoption certificates are available from the General Register Office for Northern Ireland, Oxford House, 49–55 Chichester Street, Belfast BT1 4HL (www.nidirect.gov.uk/gro).

# Republic of Ireland

The Adoption Act of 1952 introduced legal adoption in the Republic of Ireland. The Adoption Act of 2010 established a new Adoption Authority which is responsible for administering all adoptions in the Republic and also runs the National Adoption Contact Preference Register. The role of the General Register Office of Ireland is restricted to maintaining the Adopted Children Register, the creation of indexes (including 'an index to make traceable the connection between each entry in the Adopted Children Register and the corresponding entry in the register of births') and the issuing of certificates.

Irish adoption certificates can be obtained from the General Register Office, Government Offices, Convent Road, Roscommon, Republic of Ireland (www.groireland.ie).

Adoption is an emotive topic. The stories behind individual cases can be heart-rending and, for that reason, making contact is often fraught with potential difficulties. The move towards a more open approach, signposted by the various changes in legislation, reflects the changing views in society to issues such as illegitimacy but, nevertheless, anyone embarking on a search of adoption records would be well advised to approach them with caution.

## Chapter 15

# UNEXPECTED SOURCES

**M**ost of the time you will find a record of the birth, marriage or death that you want in one of the usual sources already described in this book. But there are a number of other places where you can find records of these events, as a substitute, where there is no official record, or for supplementary information if you have already found the entry you require.

There are records from which you can infer that a birth, marriage or a death has taken place by a certain date, without them actually stating the date of the event; probate records are particularly useful in this regard. Birth, marriage and death certificates of other family members can also provide vital information, and a person's marital status in a census return can help narrow down the date of their marriage, or the death of a spouse. Having said that, information in the census is often less reliable than other sources, so it should be treated with caution.

The usefulness of probate records goes beyond the obvious conclusion that if a person's will has been proved, or their estate has been administered, they must be deceased. They can provide useful information about the births, marriages and deaths of the relatives of the deceased, too. If a person's age or marital status is mentioned in a will, this will be their state at the date the will was written; for example, a daughter with a different surname from the deceased not only tells you that this was her married name, but also the fact that she was already married at that time.

It also goes without saying that anyone named as a beneficiary should still be alive when the will was written. Some probate indexes include the exact date of death, and if there was no will, the Letters of Administration taken out by the heirs will also give this information.

For ancestors who left a will in England and Wales between 1796 and 1903, the Death Duty Registers can be an unexpectedly fruitful source of information. These are at their most informative between 1815 and 1857. This is because the Inland Revenue collected its tax when a sum of money was paid out, and if the beneficiary received an annual income, rather than a lump sum, the tax would be collected every year. So, if a man left his daughters or his widow an annual income until they married, the date of the marriage would be noted in the Death Duty Register entry. If they never married, or the income was for life, the date of death would be shown, and this could be many decades after the death of the testator.

Probate indexes may also be used as finding aids to locate a death or burial entry, since they may contain information that can help you select the right one where there are several possible entries for the same name, and can also alert you to a death overseas, which will not appear in any domestic death or burial index. Since 1858 all wills and administrations for people normally resident in England and Wales are held by the Principal Probate Registry, and an incomplete set of indexes covering the years 1861–1941 is online at www.ancestry. co.uk. All of the entries in the indexes include the person's date of death.

Before 1858 the wills or administrations of any British citizens dying overseas should be recorded in the Prerogative Court of Canterbury (PCC). Wills in the PCC are available to download from www. nationalarchives.gov.uk/documentsonline for a fee, but the indexes are free to search. The administrations have not been digitised but are available at The National Archives on microfilm.

Parish registers and Bishop's Transcripts are the main sources where you will find evidence of church records of baptism, marriage and burial, but they are not the only ones. The precious parish register books were meant to be kept securely locked away in the parish chest, and may not have been taken out every time there was a baptism, marriage or burial to be recorded; in many parishes you will find an unofficial day book, containing entries that would later be written up in the official register. These are worth seeking out as a supplementary source, since they may be a more accurate record, and might even contain extra details.

You may also be lucky enough to find a sexton's burial book to supplement a burial register. This is the record of the opening of the grave, where the burial register records the religious rites of burial. Another related source for death and burial details is the information that appears on graves and tombstones. Not everyone who is buried has a gravestone, but where they do exist they sometimes contain far more information than any death or burial register. In some cases the stones themselves have been removed or have become unreadable since the recording was done, but fortunately many of these inscriptions have been recorded and published. The library of the Society of Genealogists and the Family History Library in Salt Lake City both hold excellent collections of published and unpublished records of this kind.

The National Archives holds a collection of records relating to the removal of graves and tombstones, in record series RG 37. These are twentieth-century records, but they concern graves and stones that may be much earlier in date. The records in this collection account for only a tiny proportion of burial grounds in England and Wales, and many of the records contain no names, or very few. But there are some that include many names and burial dates, and occasionally even some details of inscriptions.

The records of the National Debt Office, which administered Life Annuities 1745–57 and the Tontine of 1789, are also held in The National Archives. The records in series NDO 1-3 include many evidences of birth, marriage and death, often in the form of original certificates. They are mostly from the late eighteenth and early nineteenth centuries, and can only be consulted as original documents; unfortunately, there are no indexes.

Court records may include evidence of birth, marriage or death, where certificates have been produced as evidence, particularly in probate cases, where matters of inheritance might hinge on a person's legitimacy, and where dates of birth, marriage or death can be vital to the case. A notable example of this is the two volumes of Fleet marriages that were produced as evidence in a probate dispute and that are still in the records of the Prerogative Court of Canterbury in PROB 18/50 at The National Archives.

For an ancestor who came to Britain from overseas and became naturalised, you will find dates and places of birth in their naturalisation file in The National Archives. These are searchable by name in the online catalogue, and although the files are original documents that can only be viewed on site at Kew, you can order a copy of a naturalisation file through the Record Copying department.

Where you have been unable to find an actual birth or baptism entry, you may be able to find a record of a person's date of birth in some other kind of register. There are many kinds of institutions where a person's date of birth might be recorded on admission, and possibly the place of birth too. The admission and discharge registers that schools were required to keep from 1871 onwards are a particularly valuable source of this kind. They show the child's date of birth and the name of at least one parent or guardian, and the parent's occupation. This makes them especially useful for assigning children to the right family where they have common names. The admission and discharge registers also record the dates when each child joined and left the school, and often give extra information. If a child died while enrolled at a school, the date of death should therefore be recorded in the column showing the leaving date. Most of these records are held in county record offices, and there are several indexing projects in progress. Records for many schools in Cheshire and the London area are online at www.familysearch.org and www.ancestry.co.uk respectively.

Parishes were grouped into unions for Poor Law purposes in 1834, and each union had to provide a workhouse for its paupers. This new system created a wealth of new records too, including admission and discharge registers for the workhouses. Like school registers, these should include the dates of birth of those admitted, and in addition to the workhouses themselves, many unions also had their own schools and hospitals, also with admission and discharge registers.

The workhouses might also have Creed Registers, which record the religious denominations of inmates, and a variety of other registers, such as lists of children boarded out, which might contain dates of birth, although this is likely simply to be the year of birth, rather than the exact date. It is well worth exploring any Poor Law records available, whether those of the new system from 1834, or of the old parish system that preceded it.

The whole system of poor relief was based on the concept of settlement; everyone had a settlement, that is a parish or union that was obliged to take care of them if they were in need. This might be the place where they were born, or they may have done something to qualify for a settlement elsewhere. A woman would take her husband's place of settlement on marriage, for example. So details such as the pauper's date and place of birth, or of marriage, were crucial to the authorities in determining this, and might therefore be recorded in a variety of documents created by them. In the case of the old and new Poor Law systems any surviving records are likely to be held in the appropriate county record office.

Parishes and unions were not the only bodies that looked after the poor and the sick; charities had an important role to play, and some were parish charities, or at least worked closely with the parish authorities. Their records are worth seeking out, since they may contain birth, marriage and death dates. You can find out where records of individual charities are held by searching the National Register of Archives at www.nationalarchives.gov.uk/nra.

Occupational records of many kinds can be useful sources of information on dates of birth. Unfortunately, many records of people in the employment of private individuals do not survive, and many records give only ages on appointment, rather than exact dates of birth, but there are some exceptions. As well as records of employment with specific companies, entry into trade guilds, livery companies or even trades unions might require proof of age, and the date of birth might be recorded. The Company of Watermen and Lightermen is a good example of this; the company controlled river traffic on the Thames from the sixteenth century, and its Apprentice Binding Books 1688–1908 and Affidavit Books 1759–1897 give dates of birth for each apprentice. The records are held at the London Metropolitan Archives, and are indexed. These indexes are on microfiche and are widely available.

Railway companies were major employers from the nineteenth century, and the employment records of some companies, though not all, list dates of birth of employees. Many railway company records are held at The National Archives, and are now indexed and online at www.ancestry.co.uk.

In general there are better records for people employed in some kind of public service than for those working for private companies, although, ironically, the records of people employed in the Civil Service are generally poor. There are, however, lists of everyone employed in the General Register Office from 1836 to the mid-1880s, complete with dates and places of birth in a record book created by the department (RG 20/98). There may be similar information in the papers of other government departments, but there is no central register. A useful collection relating to the Civil Service is a 2 per cent sample of Evidences of Age 1752–1948, held at the Society of Genealogists and indexed at www.findmypast.co.uk.

Some employment records, especially where a pension is involved, may also contain a date of death. Records created by private companies will vary enormously, and may not contain any useful genealogical information, but are worth seeking out if you know the name of the company for whom an ancestor worked. You can search the National Register of Archives www.nationalarchives.gov.uk/nra to find where any surviving records are kept.

Birth, baptism, marriage, death and burial registers of armed forces personnel and their families have been dealt with elsewhere (see Chapter 9), but there are further military and naval records that provide information on births, marriages and deaths. Many individual service records contain the date of birth of the man or, in some more recent records, the woman who served, although many Army attestation papers state only an age in years and months. These ages or birthplaces need to be treated with some caution, however, as they may not be accurate.

There were incentives to give a false age on joining the service; some underage boys claimed to be 18 to when they joined up, and some older men adjusted their age down by a few years so that they would not be turned away as too old. James Calderhead was born in 1900, but he joined the Army in 1914 and again in 1915, giving his age as 18. On both occasions he was found out and discharged within a few months. Between these two attempts he also signed up with the Royal Marines, who discovered his deception and turned him away even more quickly than the Army. In 1916 he successfully joined the Royal Navy, still claiming to be 18, and this time he was accepted and served for the rest of the First World War.

All four records are held in The National Archives, and although the Army and Marine records are annotated with his correct age, there is nothing in the Navy record to indicate that he was two years younger than he claimed to be. He was not by any means the only person who ever joined up giving a false age. There are many other examples where only further research on individuals shows ages on service records to be inaccurate, and it is not unknown for young men to use the birth or baptism certificate of an older brother of the same name, but who died in infancy, to join the armed forces. In many cases, however, no documentary evidence would be required, and the information given by a recruit would be taken at face value.

From the late nineteenth century surviving Army service records may give the date and place of a soldier's marriage, and the births of his children. This is particularly helpful where a soldier's children were born outside England and Wales, and do not appear in the regimental registers of births, or in the Chaplains' Returns.

Once he was in the Army, a soldier would appear in the muster rolls, which were lists of names, rather like a school attendance register. But some muster books will contain pages listing all the new recruits who have joined the regiment and the men who have been discharged during that period, complete with their dates and places of birth. A muster book of the 74th Regiment of Foot shows that new recruit William Charlton was born on 2 November 1786 in Killieshall, County Tyrone, a particularly valuable piece of information since the registers for that parish do not start until after that date.

Other regimental records, such as casualty lists, might give the dates of death of those who died in service. There are also some records of deceased soldiers' effects, where a man's personal property would be auctioned off to his comrades, often for inflated amounts, and the proceeds given to his widow or other dependants.

Records that appear to relate only to members of the armed forces can also be of use in tracking down civilian events. The Navy Chaplains' registers held at The National Archives are a good example of this. This is a collection of 145 baptism, marriage and burial registers dating from 1845 to 1998, from naval establishments all over the world. They contain many records of civilian events, particularly overseas, where the Navy chapel might be the most convenient place for an expatriate British family to have their children baptised. Even within Britain civilian employees in naval dockyards and their families might appear in the registers of the dockyard church.

The Commonwealth War Graves Commission website is a well-known source of information on the deaths of servicemen and women during the First and Second World Wars, but it also contains some civilian deaths too. In both conflicts there are deaths of merchant navy personnel, some of whom were in the Royal Naval Reserve or Royal Naval Volunteer Reserve, but others are simply described as mercantile marine, merchant navy, fishing fleet and so on. For the Second World War only there are entries for civilian casualties as a result of enemy action, so if an ancestor was killed in a bombing raid, or as a result of injuries sustained in one, they should be listed there. For the servicemen and women whose deaths are recorded on the site, you can sometimes find extra information in the printed Imperial War Graves reports from which the databases on the website were created.

*Kensal Green Cemetery.* (Charles Knight, *London,* n.d.)

Newspapers and other printed sources can provide valuable information. They are not primary sources, and are therefore often dismissed as unreliable. While this is certainly true, finding a birth notice or an obituary or some other record in a newspaper might be the means by which you find out the date and place of an event, which you can then locate in the original church record or civil register. Like probate records, notices in newspapers can also be a useful way to find out about events that occurred overseas, and which you might not have found otherwise. These items are not confined to birth, marriage and death notices, but also obituaries, reports on funerals and some papers even listed the week's interments in the local cemetery.

Cemetery records themselves have often been difficult to use in the past because of the lack of available indexes, and the difficulty of knowing where an ancestor might be buried. Some cemetery burials are among the National Burial Index material online at www.findmypast.co.uk, but the major source is the large and increasing number of burials indexed at www.deceasedonline.co.uk. There is a charge for viewing the full record, but the indexes are free.

*Chapter 16*

# ACCESSING THE RECORDS

The biggest challenge facing family historians and others who seek to use the birth, marriage and death records created over the past five centuries by a variety of ecclesiastical and civil authorities has always been the problem of access.

In the twentieth century the situation was made much easier thanks to a process of centralisation, and in the first decade of the twenty-first century, the Internet has improved matters still further. However, online access has brought with it a whole new set of problems. The whereabouts of a parish register was previously a question of geography or administrative history, but the digital age has removed all that and has undoubtedly complicated matters. Access may be easier in most respects but knowing which database to search is by no means a straightforward matter, and with the main commercial websites competing to obtain the most useful databases for their subscribers, it becomes increasingly difficult to keep track of where to find what you're looking for.

And it's not always clear exactly what you are searching when you access a given database. You may believe that you're carrying out a comprehensive search of the records of a particular parish but are you necessarily searching *all* the records of that parish or is the database's coverage limited? The modern researcher needs, more than ever before, to read the small print.

Despite these concerns, access to parish registers and civil registration records is unquestionably continuing to improve and it's likely that the most significant family history collections to be made available online over the next decade will be the records of our ancestors' vital events.

## Civil Registration

Access to the civil registration records held by the General Register Office of England and Wales is controlled by statute. Detailed information from the registers can only be provided in the form of a certified copy, i.e. a certificate. There is currently no online access to the General Register Office's records and no official online access to their indexes.

There are two methods of obtaining copy certificates: online, by post or by telephone from the General Register Office or (for locally registered events only) in person through the local registration service. Copy certificates from the General Register Office's entire collection of birth, marriage and death records, including the numerous overseas and military registers, can be ordered online, for a fee, at www. gro.gov.uk/gro/content/certificates/default.asp.

General Register Office certificates are only available from the General Register Office. The fee payable (currently £9.25 per certificate) is set by statutory instrument – you should treat any website offering to supply certificates at higher prices with extreme caution.

Each event registered by the General Register Office has a unique reference – known as the GRO reference. For births, marriages and deaths registered in England and Wales between 1 July 1837 and 31 December 1983, this reference consists of six parts:

- The name of the person
- The name of the registration district in which the event was registered
- The year of registration
- The quarter of registration (January–March, April–June, July–September or October–December)
- A volume number
- A page number

More recent records and other events, such as overseas registrations, have different means of reference.

It is not necessary to know the GRO reference for an event in order to obtain a copy certificate, but it is highly advisable, and with the proliferation of websites offering access to the General Register Office's indexes, it is almost always possible to find the reference that you need.

## Online Access

The General Register Office has long-term plans to create an online index to their own records. Rather than relying on the contemporary indexes, which are lacking some important details in the early years and are known to be flawed, this would be an entirely new index, compiled from the entries in the registers themselves, and would include such details as the mother's maiden name for births, the spouse's name for marriages and the age of the deceased for deaths – all from the start of civil registration in 1837.

Meanwhile, a number of non-official websites have filled the gap. FreeBMD (www.freebmd.org.uk) is run entirely by volunteers. The aim is 'to transcribe the Civil Registration index of births, marriages and deaths for England and Wales, and to provide free Internet access to the transcribed records'. Coverage on the FreeBMD website is not yet complete but, at the time of writing, records of births up to 1938, marriages to 1951 and deaths to 1950 (each allowing for a few gaps) are searchable on the website.

FindMyPast (www.findmypast.co.uk) is a commercial website that provides access to a vast range of family history sources. In their Births, Marriages and Deaths section you can search the General Register Office's indexes from 1837–2006 (to 2005 only for marriages). Ancestry (www.ancestry.com or www.ancestry.co.uk) is the world's biggest genealogy website. The General Register Office's indexes from 1837–2005 are fully searchable on Ancestry, using the FreeBMD data up to 1915. The Genealogist (www.thegenealogist.co.uk) is another commercial website, which has full coverage of the marriage indexes from 1837–2005. Births are covered from 1973–2005 and deaths from 1984.

GenesReunited (www.genesreunited.co.uk) also offers full access to the complete run of General Register Office indexes from 1837–2006 (marriages up to 2005 only). Family Relatives (www.familyrelatives. com) provides limited access to the General Register Office's indexes.

Records from 1866–1920 and from 1984–2005 are fully covered, while those for the intervening years are only partially indexed.

Microfiche copies of the General Register Office's indexes are available at seven locations: Birmingham Central Library, Bridgend Reference and Information Library, British Library, City of Westminster Archives Centre, London Metropolitan Archives, Greater Manchester County Record Office and Plymouth Central Library. These records include indexes to more recent events.

The system established by the General Register Office means that there should always be two copies of each registered event; one held centrally by the General Register Office and the other, the original, kept by the local registrar. Over the years there have been many changes to the boundaries and the names of the registration districts which makes tracking down the current whereabouts of a particular register less straightforward than it might otherwise be.

An up to date list of Local Register Offices in England and Wales, giving contact details, is maintained on the GENUKI website at www. ukbmd.org.uk/genuki/reg/regoff.html. An accompanying list of Registration Districts in England and Wales (1837–1984) (www. ukbmd.org.uk/genuki/reg/index.html) provides the historical background which should enable you to identify the present location of any given register.

The GRO reference is of no use to the local registration service but the fact that an entry has been found in the General Register Office's indexes should, in theory at least, always mean that an original birth or death record is held locally.

The situation with marriages is very different as only the records of civil marriage ceremonies are likely to be held at the local register office. However, post-1837 marriage registers, whether those of the Church of England, other Protestant congregations, Roman Catholics or Jewish communities, are identical to the records held by the General Register Office. If a record of a marriage has been identified using the General Register Office's indexes, it should be possible in most instances to access these original locally held copies as an alternative to purchasing a certified copy.

The UKBMD website (www.ukbmd.org.uk) is co-ordinating a number of projects where the local registration service, often in partnership with the relevant family history society, has produced (or is in the process of producing) indexes to their records.

The following regions have indexes that are fully part of the UKBMD service: Bath, Berkshire, Cheshire, Cumbria, Lancashire, North Wales, Staffordshire, West Midlands, Wiltshire and Yorkshire. The indexes have all been developed using the same software and can be searched collectively in the UKBMD Multi-Region Search site (www.ukbmdsearch.org.uk).

In addition to these regional databases, UKBMD also provides links to the ever-increasing number of websites operated by local councils: Barnsley, Cambridgeshire, Darlington, County Durham, Gateshead, Gloucestershire, the Isle of Wight, Kent, Kingston upon Thames, Newcastle upon Tyne, North Lincolnshire, North Tyneside, Northumberland, Sheffield, South Tyneside, Sunderland, Tees Valley, Tower Hamlets, Warwickshire and Wrexham; all of these have some degree of online access to their records. The north east of England is particularly well served and a separate website, North East BMD (www.northeastbmd.org.uk), provides a 'gateway' service to the various local BMD sites in the area.

The majority of these websites include links to online ordering systems, allowing you to buy copy certificates of any of the entries in their indexes online, from the comfort of your own home.

## Parish Registers

Prior to the passing of the 1929 Parochial Registers and Records Measure, almost all Church of England parish registers were held at the local parish church, under conditions imposed by Section V of Rose's 1812 Act, 'safely and securely kept in a dry, well-painted Iron Chest ... which said Chest containing the said Books shall be con-stantly kept locked in some dry, safe and secure Place'.

The 1929 Act introduced an entirely new concept, ordering that 'the Bishop of every diocese shall have power to establish a diocesan record office, either at the same place as that at which the diocesan registry is situate or at some other place selected by him'. The Act went on to say that once the diocesan record office was set up, ministers would be able 'with the consent of the bishop and the parochial church council' to deposit:

  (i) any register books of baptisms, marriages or burials which are in his power and custody, not being books in actual use for the purpose of making entries therein; or

  (ii) any deeds or documents of value as historical records or as evidence of legal rights which are in his custody ...

While the Act fell short of ordering ministers to deposit their registers, many saw the advantages of doing so, and from the 1930s onwards large numbers of Church of England parish registers, along with a wide range of other parochial material, began to be deposited in the repositories of the new diocesan record offices, improving public access to the registers beyond recognition. Some churches were reluctant to give up their registers which they saw as a vital part of the parish's history, while many ministers were concerned about losing the income generated by the occasional requests for copies of baptismal and other certificates.

In 1978 a new Parochial Registers and Records Measure was passed with the aim of ensuring that the wealth of information recorded in the millions of documents still stored in parish churches was properly preserved and maintained for future generations. Among the many duties imposed on the Church of England was a requirement that 'all non-current registers and records which are over 100 years old must be deposited in the Diocesan Record Office'.

This condition has by and large been observed and the vast majority of pre-twentieth century parish registers are now accessible at the relevant diocesan record office – which in most cases is also the county record office.

The National Index of Parish Registers (published by the Society of Genealogists) is a comprehensive guide to the whereabouts of the surviving registers of the Church of England as well as any known Protestant Nonconformist and Roman Catholic congregations. The various volumes are arranged on a county basis and, for each parish, give details of the years covered by the registers as well as identifying any known gaps.

*The Phillimore Atlas and Index of Parish Registers,* edited by Cecil Humphery-Smith (3rd edn, 2002), gives less detailed information but is nevertheless an essential tool for the serious family historian. Each county is covered by a map showing the location of each of the ancient parishes as well as a topographical map dating from the 1830s and an alphabetical list of the parishes. The lists provide basic information about the surviving registers for each parish.

Over the years, and in the nineteenth century in particular, antiquarians and others with an active interest in genealogy and local history have taken on the enormous task of transcribing and indexing parish registers. W P Phillimore published indexes to marriages in 1,200 parishes from all around the coutry; the Harleian Society produced 89 volumes of parish registers, mostly from London and Middlesex; and the Yorkshire Archaeological Society has published 177 volumes of Yorkshire registers. Registers of many other counties were transcribed and published by local societies in the late nineteenth and early twentieth centuries. In recent years a number of family history societies have produced county wide indexes to the baptisms, marriages and burials in their areas of interest. The GENUKI website (www.genuki.org.uk) is an excellent source of information relating to published registers and indexes and provides an unrivalled guide to family and local history resources for all parts of Britain and Ireland.

The Library of the Society of Genealogists in London has a policy of collecting, where possible, copies of all known published parish register transcripts and indexes. The Society of Genealogists also has a large collection of microfilms of original parish registers and Bishop's Transcripts. Their holdings can be fully searched at www.sog.org.uk/sogcat/sogcat.shtml.

Although the Parochial Registers legislation that was passed in 1929 and 1978 undeniably improved public access to parish records, searching the individually maintained registers of nearly 12,000 Church of England parishes was never an easy task – despite the efforts of the antiquarians and parish register societies.

## Online Access
The first organisation to take proactive steps towards collating and indexing this material was the Church of Jesus Christ of Latter-Day

Saints (LDS), better known as the Mormons. The LDS Church first started collecting genealogical information relating to their members as long ago as the 1840s, and in 1894, the Genealogical Society of Utah (GSU) was formed to oversee the church's interests in family history research. The first records were microfilmed by the GSU in 1938 and the amount of material collected by the Mormons has continued to increase ever since.

In 1969, the church began its 'controlled extraction program' with the aim of transcribing and indexing key information from parish registers and other vital records worldwide, and the International Genealogical Index (IGI) was born. Intense public interest in the online launch of the IGI as part of the FamilySearch website in May 1999 caused the site to crash within a few hours. At the time of the launch, the website included more than 600 million records.

*Salt Lake City.* (Printed ephemera – authors' collection)

In the latest version of FamilySearch (www.familysearch.org) the records are divided into 688 collections. This includes a significant number of records that index English and Welsh parish register material. The 'England Births and Christenings, 1538–1975' database includes 67 million records. There are also 15 million deaths and burials (1538–1991) and a similar number of marriages (1538–1973). Many of these records were originally part of the 'controlled extraction program'.

Certain English counties have their own individual indexes in FamilySearch, developed in partnership with the relevant county record office. For Cheshire, there are no fewer than nine databases including indexes to parish registers, Bishop's Transcripts, Nonconformist records and marriage bonds and allegations – over 6.5 million records in all.

The coverage of Norfolk is extensive but in this case the records have not been indexed; instead access is provided to fully scanned digital images of the registers, allowing users to search for records themselves. The collection is estimated to include 76 per cent of Norfolk's surviving parish registers. FamilySearch also includes smaller collections of registers for Cornwall, Durham, Northumberland and Westmorland.

As a result of the GSU's ambitious filming project, the LDS church now provides access to large numbers of parish registers (often the Bishop's Transcripts) through the worldwide network of Family History Centers. To find out whether the registers for a particular parish have been filmed, search the Family History Library Catalog at www.familysearch.org/eng/Library/FHLC/frameset_fhlc.asp.

Copies of any films produced by the GSU can be ordered to view at any Family History Center (www.familysearch.org/eng/library/FHC/frameset_fhc.asp). The London Family History Centre, 64–8 Exhibition Road, London SW7 2PA is the largest in Britain and keeps a significant collection of British parish register microfilms on site. Their catalogue can be searched at www.londonfhc.org/content/catalogue.

The Church of Jesus Christ of Latter-Day Saints is also responsible for the invaluable website England Jurisdictions 1851 (http://maps.familysearch.org/). The site features a searchable database of English placenames linked to interactive maps of the country, showing county, parish and civil registration boundaries, together with a number of other important jurisdictions. The database also provides links to the Family History Library Catalog.

The IGI and FamilySearch are not comprehensive and it should always be remembered that they are merely indexes; they may contain errors and there will almost certainly be information in the original record that is not included in the index. As a general rule, researchers are always advised to seek out original records, rather than relying on information taken from an index.

Due to the Mormons' religious beliefs, records of deaths and burials were not, as a rule, included in the IGI (this is not the case with the new FamilySearch website which includes large numbers of death and burial records) and in 2001, in an attempt to fill the gap, the Federation of Family History Societies launched the National Burial Index (NBI). The third and latest edition of the NBI, which was published on CD-Rom in 2010, includes the records of 18.4 million burials. Coverage varies around the country with over 2 million records from the West Riding of Yorkshire, over 1 million from Suffolk and just under 1 million from Essex, but only 4,000 from Devon and 6,000 from Westmorland.

Some of the records from the NBI (approximately 7 million burials) are available to search on the FindMyPast website (see below).

As well as being the largest database as far as parish registers are concerned, FamilySearch has the added attraction of being entirely free to use, but a number of commercial websites also have significant collections of parish register material.

Foremost among these is Ancestry (www.ancestry.co.uk) which in recent years has opened up some vast parish-register collections to their subscribers. Four databases in particular are worthy of mention:

- London – births and baptisms (1538–1906), marriages (1538–1921) and death and burials (1538–1980)
- Liverpool – births and baptisms (1659–1906), marriages (1659–1921) and deaths and burials (1659–1988)
- West Yorkshire – births and baptisms (1538–1906), marriages (1538–1921) and deaths and burials (1538–1985)

- Dorset – births and baptisms (1813–1906), marriages (1813–1921) and deaths and burials (1813–2001)

Ancestry also provides online access to Pallot's Marriage Index, which was originally compiled during the nineteenth century, and includes 1.5 million records, mainly from London and Middlesex. Access is to digital images of the original index cards and not to the marriage registers themselves.

A number of miscellaneous indexes make up the remainder of Ancestry's 'Birth, Marriage and Death' section. Some of these represent significant collections of records: the England & Wales Christening Records (1530–1906) and Marriage Records (1538–1940) are, in effect, the entries for England and Wales taken from the second edition of the former LDS database, the British Isles Vital Records Index (BIVRI). As with the IGI, coverage is patchy but as the indexes include over 10 million records the database is well worth searching. In August 2008 the LDS announced that they were 'in the process of adding' the records from the BIVRI to FamilySearch.

The FindMyPast website (www.findmypast.co.uk) also provides access to large numbers of parish register indexes, the full list of which can be found at www.findmypast.co.uk/helpadvice/knowledge-base/parish-records/index.jsp. FindMyPast's Parish Records Collection comprises around 100 separate databases, many of which represent significant collections.

The City of London Burials Index contains the records of more than ½ million burials that took place in and around the City of London, mostly from 1813 to the early 1850s, although the index is gradually being expanded, working backwards to 1754.

The Derbyshire Registrars Marriages index is of particular interest as it covers 645,071 marriages, from 1,062 Derbyshire churches and chapels – all of which took place *after* 1837.

The West Middlesex Marriages Index includes over 80,000 burials from the western part of the ancient county of Middlesex, extending as far east as Chelsea, Fulham and Kensington.

More than ½ million baptisms from 13 parishes centred on the dockyards in London's East End are covered by the London Dockland

Baptisms, which also extends south of the River Thames to include the parishes of Bermondsey and Newington.

The Cornwall Baptisms database covers over 1 million baptisms from more than 300 Cornwall parishes, including several Nonconformist registers.

An excellent free online resource is provided by the Online Parish Clerks (www.onlineparishclerks.org.uk). Run entirely by volunteers, this ambitious project began in Cornwall in 2000 and aims to 'provide free information about a parish, its people and history, to assist family historians'. There are currently ten counties associated with the project: Cornwall, Devon, Dorset, Essex, Hampshire, Lancashire, Somerset, Sussex, Warwickshire and Wiltshire. Each of these counties has a website providing links to information about individual parishes, which often include transcripts of parish registers.

Copies of transcripts and indexes of parish registers can be found all over the Internet and an intelligent Google search will often pay dividends.

## Nonconformist and Other Registers

The 2 Non-parochial Registers Commissions of 1840 and 1857 resulted in the bringing together of more than 7,000 non-parochial registers, the vast majority of which came from the congregations of Protestant Dissenters.

For more than a hundred years, the registers were held by the General Register Office, who used them to issue certificates of births, marriages and deaths for legal purposes. Then, in the early 1960s, they were transferred to the Public Record Office, now The National Archives, where they were catalogued in five distinct record series:

- RG 4 – Registers of Births, Marriages and Deaths surrendered to the Non-parochial Registers Commissions of 1837 and 1857
- RG 5 – Birth Certificates from the Presbyterian, Independent and Baptist Registry and from the Wesleyan Methodist Metropolitan Registry
- RG 6 – Society of Friends' Registers, Notes and Certificates of Births, Marriages and Burials

- RG 7 – Registers of Clandestine Marriages and of Baptisms in the Fleet Prison, King's Bench Prison, the Mint and the May Fair Chapel
- RG 8 – Registers of Births, Marriages and Deaths surrendered to the Non-parochial Registers Commission of 1857, and other registers and church records

The last of these collections includes registers that, for one reason or another, were left unauthenticated by the Commissions.

This entire collection of registers has been digitised and indexed and is available to search online (for a fee) at www.bmdregisters. co.uk.

Not all registers were surrendered to the Commissions. Many (particularly those belonging to congregations that were no longer in existence) were lost and many more were retained by the congregations.

## Roman Catholic Records

The vast majority of Roman Catholic registers remain in the care of the individual churches. The Catholic Family History Society (www.catholic-history.org.uk/cfhs/index.htm) has transcribed and indexed many of the surviving registers and copies of these can now be seen at the Catholic National Library, St Michael's Abbey, Farnborough Road, Farnborough, Hants GU14 7NQ (www.catholic-library.org.uk).

Up until 1918, the Catholic Church in England and Wales was organised by missions, rather than parishes, and the registers were often taken from mission to mission as the priests moved around the country. A small number of these registers is now held by the Westminster Diocesan Archives, 16a Abingdon Road, Kensington, London W8 6AF (http://rcdowarchives.blogspot.com).

The best guide to Roman Catholic registers is Michael Gandy's *Catholic Missions and Registers, 1700–1880* (1998). This six-volume reference work lists all the known surviving Roman Catholic registers, their covering dates and whereabouts.

Vol. 3 of the National Index of Parish Registers (see above) covers Sources for Roman Catholic and Jewish Genealogy and Family History Research.

## Jewish Records

The Non-parochial Registers Commissions did not request the surrender of registers held by Jewish synagogues and for that reason, most of the surviving Jewish registers remain in the care of the synagogues. The biggest single collection of records is that of the London Beth Din (the Court of the Chief Rabbi) which has recently been deposited at the London Metropolitan Archives, 40 Northampton Road, London EC1R 0HB (www.cityoflondon.gov.uk/lma). These records can be searched via their online catalogue (http://search.lma.gov.uk/opac_lma/index.htm). The Church of Jesus Christ of Latter-Day Saints has microfilmed a number of Jewish birth, marriage and death records.

The Jewish Genealogical Society of Great Britain (www.jgsgb.org.uk) provides guidance and advice on all aspects of Jewish family history research.

# APPENDIX: THE LEGISLATION

This section is designed to provide an overview of the most important legislation relating to the recording of birth, marriage and death records in England and Wales since 1538.

A familiarity with the wording of the legislation is vital for a proper understanding of the impact of the legislation but there isn't space to include the full text of the various Acts here. For a full transcript of the above-mentioned Acts, as well as many others of interest to social and family historians, see http://freepages.genealogy.rootsweb.ancestry.com/~framland/acts/actind.htm. For current legislation see the official government website, www.legislation.gov.uk.

| | |
|---|---|
| 5 September 1538 | Thomas Cromwell issues his 'Order For Keeping Parish Registers'. |

*[Translated into modern English] Item that you and every parson, vicar or curate in this diocese shall for every church, keep one book or register wherein you shall write the day and year of every wedding, christening and burying made within your parish for your time, and so every man succeeding you likewise. And shall there insert every person's name that shall be so wedded, christened or buried. And for the safe keeping of the same book, the parish shall be bound to provide, out of their common charges, one sure [secure] coffer with two locks and keys, whereof the one to remain with you, and the other with the said wardens, wherein the said book shall be laid up. Which book, you shall every Sunday take forth and in the presence of the said wardens, or one of them, write and record in the same all the weddings, christenings and buryings made the whole week before. And that done, to lay up the*

*book in the said coffer as before. And for every time that the same shall be omitted, the party that shall be in the fault thereof shall forfeit to the said church 3s 4d to be employed on the reparation of the same church.*

| | |
|---|---|
| 25 October 1597–1603 | Elizabeth I issues a further Order (which, shortly after Elizabeth's death, is embodied in the seventieth canon of 1603) requiring copies of existing registers to be made in new parchment books and also instituting Bishop's Transcripts. |

*In every parish Church and Chapel within this Realm shall be provided one parchment book at the charge of the Parish, wherein shall be written the day and year of every Christening, Wedding, and Burial which have been in that Parish since the time that the Law was first made in that behalf, so far as the ancient books thereof can be procured, but especially since the beginning of the reign of the late Queen ...*

*And the Churchwardens shall once every year within one month after the five-and-twentieth day of March, transmit unto the Bishop of the Diocese, or his Chancellor, a true copy of the names of all persons christened, married or buried in the Parish in the year before ... and the certain days and months in which such christening, marriage and burial was had, to be subscribed with the hands of the said Minister and Churchwardens to the end the same may faithfully be preserved in the Registry of the said Bishop, which certificate shall be received without fee. And if the Minister and Churchwardens shall be negligent in performance of anything herein contained it shall be lawful for the Bishop or his Chancellor to convent them and proceed against every of them as contemners of this our Constitution.*

| | |
|---|---|
| 4 January 1644/5 | An 'ordinance' is passed during the first period of the English Civil War concerning 'Register Books for Births, and Marriages and Burials'. |

*And it is further Ordained by the Authority aforesaid, That there shall be provided at the charge of every*

166

*Parish or Chappelry in this Realm of England, and Dominion of Wales, a fair Register Book of Velim, to be kept by the Minister and other Officers of the Church; and that the Names of all Children Baptized, and of their Parents and of the time of their Birth and Baptizing, shall be written and set down by the Minister therein; and also the Names of all Persons Married there, and the time of their Marriage; and also the Names of all Persons Buried in that Parish, and the time of their Death and Burial: And that the said Book shall be shewed by such as keep the same, to all persons reasonably desiring to search for the Birth, Baptizing, Marriage, or Burial of any person therein Registred, and to take a Copy, or procure a Certificate thereof.*

24 August 1653

Parliament passes 'An Act touching Marriages and the Registring thereof; and also touching Births and Burials', introducing a form of civil registration and ordering that all marriages were to be performed before a Justice of the Peace.

*Be it Enacted by the authority of this present Parliament, That whosoever shall agree to be married within the Commonwealth of England, after the Nine and twentieth day of September, in the year One thousand six hundred fifty three, shall (one and twenty days at least before such intended Marriage) deliver in writing, or cause to be so delivered unto the Register (hereafter appointed by this Act) for the respective Parish where each party to be married liveth, the names, surnames, additions, and places of aboad of the parties so to be married, and of their Parents, Guardians or Overseers; All which the said Register shall publish or cause to be published, three several Lords-days then next following, at the close of the morning Exercise, in the publique Meeting place commonly called the Church or Chappel; or (if the parties so to be married shall desire it) in the Market-place next to the said Church or Chappel, on three Market-days in three several weeks next following, between the hours of eleven and two ...*

167

*And it is further Enacted, That the Man and Woman having made sufficient proof of the consent of their Parents or Guardians as aforesaid, and expressed their consent unto Marriage, in the maner and by the words aforesaid, before such Justice of Peace in the presence of two or more credible Witnesses; the said Justice of Peace may and shall declare the said Man and Woman to be from thenceforth Husband and Wife; and from and after such consent so expressed, and such declaration made, the same (as to the form of Marriage) shall be good and effectual in Law; And no other Marriage whatsoever within the Commonwealth of England, after the 29th of September, in the year One thousand six hundred fifty three, shall be held or accompted a Marriage according to the Laws of England . . .*

*And that a true and just accompt may be always kept, as well of Publications, as of all such Marriages, and also of the Births of Children, and Deaths of all sorts of persons within this Commonwealth; Be it further Enacted, That a Book of good Vellum or Parchment shall be provided by every Parish, for the Registring of all such Marriages, and of all Births of Children, and Burials of all sorts of people within every Parish; for the safe keeping of which Book, the Inhabitants and Housholders of every Parish chargeable to the relief of the poor, or the greater part of them present, shall on or before the Two and twentieth day of September, in the year One thousand six hundred fifty three, make choice of some able and honest person (such as shall be sworn and approved by one Justice of the Peace in that Parish, Division or County, and so signified under his hand in the said Register-Book) to have the keeping of the said Book, who shall therein fairly enter in writing all such Publications, Marriages, Births of Children, and Burials of all sorts of persons, and the Names of every of them, and the days of the moneth and year of Publications, Marriages, Births and Burials, and the Parents, Guardians or Overseers names . . . And the person so elected, approved and sworn, shall be called the Parish-Register . . .*

168

*And all Register-Books for Marriages, Births and Burials already past, shall be delivered into the hands of the respective Registers appointed by this Act, to be kept as Records.*

| 1660 | The 'Confirmation of Marriages Act' is passed, legalising, |

*all marriages within any of his Majesties Dominions since the same first day of May in the yeare of our Lord One thousand six hundred forty two had or solemnized according to the direction or true intent of any Act or Ordinance or reputed Act or Ordinance of one or both Houses of Parliament, or of any Convention sitting at Westminster under the Name Stile or Title of a Parliament*

| 1678 | 'An Act for Burying in Woollen' is passed, requiring burials to be in English woollen shrouds with sworn affidavits as evidence and instructing the clergy to keep records in the parish registers. |

*VII. And it is hereby further enacted, That the Parson or Minister of every Parish shall keep a Register in a Book to be provided at the Charge of the Parish, and make a true Entry of all Burials within his Parish, and of all Affidavits brought to him as aforesaid, within the Time limited as aforesaid; and where no such Affidavit shall be brought to him within such Time, that he enter a Memorial thereof in the said Registry, against the Name of the Party interred, and of the Time when he notified the same to the Churchwardens or Overseers of the Poor.*

| 1695 | 'An Act for Granting to His Majesty certain Rates and Duties upon Marriages, Births and Burials, and upon Batchelors and Widowers, for the Term of Five Years, for Carrying on the War against France with Vigour' is passed, introducing a tax on entries in parish registers. |

*And be it enacted ... That from and after the First day of May, in the year of our Lord One thousand six hundred ninety and five, for and during the term of Five Years ... there shall be raised, and levied and paid to his Majesty ... the several and respective Duties and Sums of Money herein after mentioned ...*

1696 'An Act for the enforcing the Laws which restrain Marriages without Licence or Banns, and for the better registring Marriages, Births, and Burials' is passed amending the above Act of 1695 and ordering that the births of *all* children should be registered, whether they are baptised or not.

*V ... be it enacted ... That from and after the four and twentieth Day of June, which shall be in the Year one thousand six hundred ninety and six, the Parents of every Child, which shall at any Time be born after the said Day and Year ... shall within five Days after such Birth give Notice to the respective Rector, Vicar, Curate, or Clerk of the Parish or Place where such Child was born, of the Day of the Birth of every such Child ... the which said Rector, Vicar, Curate, or Clerk of the Parish, or their Substitutes, are hereby required, during the Continuance of the said Act, to take an exact and true Account, and keep a distinct Register of all and every Person or Persons so born in his or their respective Parishes or Precincts, and not christened ...*

1753 'An Act for the better preventing of clandestine Marriages' (better known as Hardwicke's Marriage Act) is passed ordering that all marriages should take place in a church or chapel after banns or by licence; that they should be recorded in registers with numbered pages; that the names of two witnesses should be recorded and that Quakers and Jews were exempted.

*VIII Be it enacted, That if any Person shall, from and after the said twenty-fifth Day of March in the Year one thousand seven hundred and fifty-four, solemnize Matrimony in any other Place than a Church or Publick Chapel, where Banns have been usually*

*published, unless by Special Licence from the
Archbishop of Canterbury; or shall solemnize
Matrimony without Publication of Banns, unless
Licence of Marriage be first had and obtained from
same Person or Persons having Authority to grant the
same, every Person knowingly and wilfully so
offending, and being lawfully convicted thereof, shall be
deemed and adjudged to be guilty of Felony … and all
Marriages solemnized from and after the twenty-fifth
Day of March in the Year one thousand seven hundred
and fifty-four, in any other Place than a Church or
such Publick Chapel, unless by Special Licence as
aforesaid, or that shall be solemnized with Publication
of Banns, or Licence of Marriage from a Person or
Persons having Authority to grant the same first had
and obtained, shall be null and void to all Intents and
Purposes whatsoever.*

*XIV And for preventing undue Entries and Abuses in
Registers of Marriages; Be it enacted … That on or
before the twenty-fifth Day of March in the Year one-
thousand seven hundred and fifty-four, and from Time
to Time afterwards as there shall be Occasion, the
Church-wardens and Chapel-wardens of every Parish
or Chapelry shall provide proper Books of Vellum, or
good and durable Paper, in which all Marriages and
Banns of Marriage respectively, there published or
solemnized, shall be registered, and every Page thereof
shall be marked at the Top, with the Figure of the
Number of every such Page, beginning at the second
Leaf with Number one; and every Leaf or Page so
numbered, shall be ruled with Lines at proper and
equal Distances from each other, or as near as may be;
and all Banns and Marriages published or celebrated in
any Church or Chapel, or within any such Parish or
Chapelry, shall be respectively entered, registered,
printed, or written upon or as near as conveniently
may be to such ruled Line, and shall be signed by the
Parson, Vicar, Minister or Curate, or by some other
Person in his Presence and by his Direction; and such
Entries shall be made as aforesaid, on or near such
Lines in successive Order, where the Paper is not*

*damaged or decayed, by Accident or Length of Time, until a new Book shall be thought proper or necessary to be provided for the same Purposes, and then the Directions aforesaid shall be observed in every such new Book; and all Books provided as aforesaid shall be deemed to belong to every such Parish or Chapel respectively, and shall be carefully kept and preserved for publick Use.*

*XV And ... Be it enacted, That from and after the twenty-fifth Day of March in the Year one thousand seven hundred and fifty-four, all Marriages shall be solemnized in the Presence of two or more credible Witnesses, besides the Minister who shall celebrate the same; and that immediately after the Celebration of every Marriage, an Entry thereof shall be made in such Register to be kept as aforesaid; in which Entry or Register it shall be expressed, That the said Marriage was celebrated by Banns or Licence; and if both or either of the Parties married by Licence, be under Age, with Consent of the Parents or Guardians, as the Case shall be and shall be signed by the Minister with his proper Addition, and also by the Parties married, and attested by such two Witnesses.*

*XVIII Provided likewise, That nothing in this Act contained shall extend to that Part of Great Britain called Scotland, nor to any Marriages amongst the People called Quakers, or amongst the Persons professing the Jewish Religion, where both the Parties to any such Marriage shall be of the People called Quakers, or Persons professing the Jewish Religion respectively, nor to any Marriages solemnized beyond the Seas.*

---

1783    'An Act for granting to His Majesty a Stamp duty on the Registry of Burials, Marriages, Births and Christenings' is passed, introducing a tax on parish register entries.

*That, from and after the first Day of October, one thousand seven hundred and eighty-three, there shall be charged, levied, and paid unto and for the Use of his Majesty, his Heirs and Successors, the new Duty following; (that is to say,) Upon the Entry of any Burial, Marriage, Birth or Christening, in the Register of any Parish, Precinct or Place in Great Britain, Stamp-duty of three Pence.*

| | |
|---|---|
| 28 June 1812 | 'An Act for the better regulating and preserving Parish and other Registers of Births, Baptisms, Marriages, and Burials, in England', better known as Rose's Act, is passed, introducing pre-printed, pro forma parish registers. |

*Whereas the amending the Manner and Form of keeping and of preserving Registers of Baptisms, Marriages, and Burials of His Majesty's Subjects in the several Parishes and Places in England, will greatly facilitate the Proof of Pedigrees of Persons claiming to be entitled to Real or Personal Estates, and be otherwise of great public Benefit and Advantage; Be it therefore enacted ... That, from and after the Thirty first Day of December One thousand eight hundred and twelve, Registers of Public and Private Baptisms, Marriages, and Burials ... shall be made and kept by the Rector, Vicar, Curate, or Officiating Minister of every Parish ... whereon shall be printed, upon each Side of every Leaf, the Heads of Information herein required to be entered in the Registers of Baptism, Marriages and Burials respectively, and every such Entry shall be numbered progressively from the Beginning to the End of each Book, the first Entry to be distinguished by Number One; and every such Entry shall be divided from the Entry next following by a printed Line, according to the Forms contained in the Schedules hereto annexed; and every Page of every such Book shall be numbered with progressive Numbers, the first Page being marked with the Number 1. in the Middle of the upper Part of such Page, and every subsequent Page being marked in like Manner with progressive Numbers from Number 1. to the End of the Book.*

17 August 1836

'An Act for registering Births, Deaths and Marriages in England' is passed, introducing civil registration in England and Wales. 'An Act for Marriages in England' is passed on the same day.

*II And be it enacted, That it shall be lawful for His Majesty to provide a proper Office in London or Westminster, to be called 'The General Register Office', for keeping a Register of all Births, Deaths, and Marriages of His Majesty's Subjects in England, and to appoint for the said Office under the Great Seal of the United Kingdom a Registrar General of Births, Deaths, and Marriages in England ...*

*XIX And be it enacted, That the Father or Mother of any Child born, or the Occupier of every House or Tenement in England in which any Birth or Death shall happen after the said First Day of March, may, within Forty-two Days next after the Day of such Birth or within Five Days after the Day of such Death respectively, give Notice of such Birth or Death to the Registrar of the District ...*

*XXXVII And be it enacted, That the Registrar General shall cause Indexes of all the said certified Copies of the Registers to be made and kept in the General Register Office ...*

24 February 1837

'An Act to suspend for a limited Time the Operation of Two Acts passed in the last Session of Parliament, for the registering Births, Deaths, and Marriages in England, and for Marriages in England' is passed, delaying the introduction of civil registration by three months.

*Be it therefore enacted ... That ... the said Two Acts respectively shall be constructed as if the Words 'last day of June' had been inserted in the said Acts instead of the Words 'First Day of March', in every Place where the last-mentioned Words are found in the said Acts respectively ...*

| | |
|---|---|
| 30 June 1837 | 'An Act to explain and amend Two Acts for Marriages and for registering Birth Deaths and Marriages' is passed, clarifying certain aspects of the 1836 Acts. |

| | |
|---|---|
| 10 August 1840 | 'An Act for enabling Courts of Justice to admit Non-parochial Registers as Evidence of Births or Baptisms, Deaths or Burials and Marriages' is passed, retrospectively giving legal status to Nonconformist registers. |

*VI And be it enacted, That all Registers and Records deposited in the General Register Office by virtue of this Act ... shall be deemed to be in legal Custody, and shall be receivable in Evidence in all Courts of Justice ...*

| | |
|---|---|
| 28 August 1857 | 'An Act to amend the Law relating to Divorce and Matrimonial Causes in England' is passed, making divorce a realistic prospect for ordinary people for the first time. |

| | |
|---|---|
| 7 August 1874 | 'An Act for the registering of Births, Deaths, and Marriages in England' is passed, introducing some important amendments to the 1836 Acts. |

*1. In the case of every child born alive after the commencement of this Act, it shall be the duty of the father and mother of the child, and in default of the father and mother, of the occupier of the house in which to his knowledge the child is born, and of each person present at the birth, and of the person having charge of the child, to give to the registrar, within forty-two days next after such birth, information of the particulars required to be registered concerning such birth ...*

*7. In the case of an illegitimate child no person shall, as father of such child, be required to give information under this Act concerning the birth of such child, and the registrar shall not enter in the register the name of any person as father of such child, unless at the joint request of the mother and of the person acknowledging himself to be the father of such child, and such person shall in such case sign the register, together with the mother.*

| | |
|---|---|
| 4 August 1926 | 'An Act to make provision for the adoption of Infants' was passed, introducing legal adoption in England and Wales. |

*11.1 The Registrar-General shall establish and maintain at the General Register Office a register to be called the Adopted Children Register, in which shall be made such entries as may be directed to be made therein by adoption orders, but no other entries.*

*11.2 Every adoption order shall contain a direction to the Registrar-General to make in the Adopted Children Register an entry recording the adoption in the form set out in the Schedule hereto.*

*11.3 If upon any application for an adoption order there is proved to the satisfaction of the Court: the date of the birth of the infant; and the identity of the infant with a child to which any entry or entries in the Registers of Births relates; the adoption order shall contain a further direction to the Registrar-General to cause such birth, entry or entries in the Registers of Birth, to be marked with the word 'Adopted', and to include in the entry in the adoption register recording the adoption the date stated in the order of the adopted child's birth in the manner indicated in the Schedule hereto.*

# BIBLIOGRAPHY

Annal, David, *Easy Family History*, 2006

Backhurst, Marie-Louise, *Tracing Your Channel Islands Ancestors*, 2011

Benton, Tony, *Irregular Marriages in London before 1754*, 2nd edn, 2000

Bevan, Amanda, *Tracing Your Ancestors in The National Archives: The Website and Beyond*, 7th edn, 2006

Blake, Paul and Audrey Collins, *Who Was Your Granny's Granny?*, 2003

Breed, Geoffrey, *My Ancestors were Baptists*, 2007

Christian, Peter, *The Genealogist's Internet*, 4th edn, 2009

Christian, Peter and David Annal, *Census: The Expert Guide*, 2008

Clifford, David, *My Ancestors were Congregationalists*, 1997

Cox, J Charles, *Parish Registers of England*, 1910

Dixon, Barbara, *Birth and Death Certificates – England and Wales 1837 to 1969*, 1999

——, *Marriages and Certificates in England & Wales*, 2000

Durie, Bruce, *Scottish Genealogy*, 2010

Foster, Michael Whitfield, *A Comedy of Errors, or, The Marriage Records of England and Wales, 1837–1899*, 1998

——, *A Comedy of Errors, Act 2*, 2000 and 2001

Fowler, Simon, *Tracing Your Army Ancestors*, 2006

Gandy, Michael, *Catholic Missions and Registers 1700–1880*, 6 vols, 1998

Grenham, John, *Tracing Your Irish Ancestors*, 3rd edn, 2006

Guildhall Library, *The British Overseas: A Guide to Records of their Births, Baptisms, Marriages, Deaths and Burials Available in the United Kingdom*, 3rd edn, 1994

Herber, Mark, *Ancestral Trails*, 2nd edn, 2005

Higgs, Edward, *Life, Death and Statistics*, 2004

Humphery-Smith, Cecil (ed.), *The Phillimore Atlas and Index of Parish Registers*, 3rd edn, 2002

Joseph, Anthony, *My Ancestors were Jewish*, 4th edn, 2008

Langston, Brett, *A Handbook to the Civil Registration Districts of England and Wales*, 2nd edn, 2003

Maxwell, Ian, *Tracing Your Northern Irish Ancestors*, 2010

Mullett, Michael A, *Sources for the History of English Nonconformity, 1660–1830*, 1991

Narasimham, Janet, *The Manx Family Tree: a beginner's guide to records in the Isle of Man*, 2nd edn, 1994

National Archives of Scotland, *Tracing Your Scottish Ancestors*, 5th edn, 2009

Nissel, Muriel, *People Count: A History of the General Register Office*, 1987

Paton, Chris, *Researching Scottish Family History*, 2010

Probert, Rebecca, *Marriage Law and Practice in the Long Eighteenth Century: A Reassessment*, 2009

Ruston, Alan, *My Ancestors were English Presbyterians & Unitarians*, 2nd edn, 2001

Spencer, William, *Army Records: A Guide for Family Historians*, 2008

Stone, Lawrence, *The Road to Divorce: England 1530–1987*, 1990

Watts, Michael J and Christopher T Watts, *My Ancestor was in the British Army*, 1992

——, *Tracing Births, Deaths and Marriages at Sea*, 2004

Webb, Cliff, *Greater London Cemeteries and Crematoria*, 6th edn, 2007

Webb, Cliff et al., *National Index of Parish Registers*, various dates

Wiggins, Ray, *Registration Districts*, 3rd edn, 2001

# Index

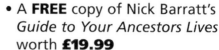